THE MI

THE ROUGH GUIDE

There are more than one hundred Rough Guide travel,
phrasebook, and music titles, covering destinations
from Amsterdam to Zimbabwe, languages
from Czech to Thai, and musics from World to
Opera and Jazz

Forthcoming titles include

Bangkok • Barbados • Japan
Jordan • Syria • Music USA
Country Music

Rough Guides on the Internet

http://www.roughguides.com

Rough Guide Credits

Text editor: Orla Duane. Series editor: Mark Ellingham
Production: Henry Iles, Susanne Hillen, Judy Pang

Publishing Information

This first edition published April 1998 by
Rough Guides Ltd, 1 Mercer St, London WC2H 9QJ.

Distributed by the Penguin Group:

Penguin Books Ltd, 27 Wrights Lane, London W8 5TZ
Penguin Books USA Inc., 375 Hudson Street, New York 10014, USA
Penguin Books Australia Ltd, 487 Maroondah Highway,
PO Box 257, Ringwood, Victoria 3134, Australia
Penguin Books Canada Ltd, 10 Alcorn Avenue,
Toronto, Ontario, Canada M4V 1E4
Penguin Books (NZ) Ltd, 182–190 Wairau Road,
Auckland 10, New Zealand

Typeset in Bembo and Helvetica to an original design by Henry Iles.
Printed in Spain by Graphy Cems.

© Nick Hanna 1998. 272pp, includes index
A catalogue record for this book is available from the British Library.
ISBN 1-85828-314-0

THE MILLENNIUM

THE ROUGH GUIDE

by Nick Hanna

Acknowledgements

I first came across millenarian movements when studying social anthropology at Sussex University twenty years ago, and I remember thinking at the time that there would be a book in it as the year 2000 approached. Little did I realise then the extent to which millennium fever would take hold in the western world, nor indeed quite what this book would involve. I have known the Rough Guides team as friends and associates for many years and, despite a mutual wish to work together, never found the right project – until now. I'd particularly like to thank Mark Ellingham for his consistent support and numerous lunches, editor Orla Duane for dealing stoically with numerous last-minute revisions, Henry Iles for his creative input, and Margaret Doyle for her proofreading.

I am also grateful to my family for their support and encouragement during the seemingly endless gestation period for this book even though the only place I travelled was in cyberspace, and to Simon and Jackie, proprietors of the Aldred Road Hotel, for their unstinting hospitality, sanctuary, and very reasonable room rates. Additionally for their help on various sections, I am indebted to my brother Mark Hanna (Web sites), Jennifer Moorhead (Palestine), Tore Indrerak Petersen (Norway) and Melissa Shales (Travel Briefs).

Finally, many thanks to all those individuals and organisations all over the world who have responded generously to requests for information.

Dedicated to my sons Luke and Oscar, who will
experience many wonders in the next millennium.

The Author

As a travel writer and photographer Nick Hanna has worked for numerous national and international newspapers and magazines and written eight guidebooks, including one that covered over 200 tropical beaches around the world. He has also written extensively on scuba diving, the marine environment, and the impact of tourism on host countries.

CONTENTS

PREFACE

The world is about to experience the biggest celebration in the history of humanity. Never mind that the millennium doesn't really start until 2001 – it is the big, round figure of 2000 that has firmly gripped the global imagination.

Thousands of parties are being planned across Europe, the Americas, Australasia and the Pacific. Monuments to the millennium – pyramids, domes, spires, towers and arches – are springing up all over the world. Beacons, fireworks, lasers and light shows will illuminate the night sky as midnight arrives in each of the planet's 24 time zones. Dawn ceremonies will mark the sunrise, whether performed by druids in Britain, drummers in New Mexico, or islanders chanting on a beach in Fiji. Festivals, parades, dance, song, music, theatre and every other art form imaginable will embrace the millennial *Zeitgeist*. Huge television screens will be erected in city squares throughout the globe and, for the first time ever, the yielding of one thousand-year epoch to another will be observed simultaneously worldwide.

Most of us will want to mark 'civilisation's most spectacular birthday' in some way. On its Web site, Rough Guides has been asking the question 'Where would you most like to be on New Year's Eve 1999?', and the replies have shown suitably unworldly ambitions. Top locales for the midnight hour, alas unattainable, were orbiting the moon and watching the terrestrial fireworks from the Space Shuttle.

Staying mostly on our own planet (though you'll find information on extra-terrestrial plans in our 'Cults' section in Contexts), this book is intended as a source of information on the events – official and otherwise – taking place in the major cities worldwide around the year 2000. We've also provided some answers to what Internet users call FAQs – Frequently Asked Questions – about whether the world really will end, whether all the computers will crash, and whether we should all be holding out for January 1, 2001.

THE MILLENNIUM

FAQs

What is the 'millennium'?

Derived from the Latin *mille* (one thousand) and *annus* (years), a millennium is a period of one thousand years. The Millennium (with a capital M), however, has a far more specific meaning for theologians and social scientists, and refers to the belief in the dawning of a new age, a 'heaven on earth', during which all strife and suffering will be abolished and peace, justice and perfect harmony will reign supreme.

For Christians the Millennium is a period when Jesus Christ will return to rule the earth for a period of one thousand years, as set out in the last book of the New Testament, the Book of Revelation. The idea of the Millennium is, in fact, much older and more far-reaching than the Christian version in Revelation, and indeed some concept of a return to paradise seems almost universal throughout human belief systems.

When does the next millennium begin?

The next millennium begins on January 1, 2001. This date relates to the Gregorian calendar, which was drawn up when Roman numerals (which do not feature a zero) were still in use. It may seem strange today, but it was a perfectly workable system, using the numerals X (10), XX (20), C (100), M (1000) and so on.

Problems with this calendar first arose when a Scythian monk, Dionysus Exiguus, introduced the AD ('Anno Domini') dating system in the late fifth century. Not having use of a zero, he dated Christ's birth as 1 AD. His error was compounded two hundred years later by a Northumbrian monk, the Venerable Bede, who created the BC system by extending Dionysus's system backwards into the years before Christ's birth. Like his predecessor, he didn't have use of a zero and so the calendar went backwards, straight from 1 AD to 1 BC. This now seems absurd, rather like counting backwards from eleven to nine while missing out ten, but it is a calendrical anomaly that has persisted for twelve centuries.

According to this system, the first year of the first millennium ran from January 1, 1 AD, to December 31, 1 AD, and the one thousandth year ran from January 1, 1000 AD, to December 31, 1000 AD, making the first day of the second millennium January 1, 1001. The start of the next millennium, therefore, will be January 1, 2001.

Most people will celebrate the eve of the new millennium on the night of December 31, 1999/January 1, 2000, even though this is technically a year too early. A similar argument has also arisen in previous centuries. On December 26, 1799, *The Times* thundered that "the present century will not terminate til 1 January, 1801...We shall not pursue this matter further...It is a silly, childish discussion and only exposes the want of brains of those who maintain a contrary opinion to that we have stated."

But today even the Old Royal Observatory at Greenwich, whilst maintaining that 2001 is the start of the next millennium, is planning to celebrate in 2000. The weight of popular opinion, not to mention sponsorship opportunities, has held sway.

"There is no need for us to argue with those who tell us it is really 2001. It is the round thousands which have the magical power; that goes back to the ancient Etruscans and the ancient Jews."
Conor Cruise O'Brien, *On the Eve of the Millennium.*

"Some have made the argument that the next millennium does not even begin until 2001, so there is no real millennial significance to the year 2000...2000 is a big round number, teeming with prophetic and apocalyptic significance for the beginning of a new age."
Philip Lamy, *Millennium Rage.*

Why are people saying the millennium has already happened?

This is because of the confusion surrounding Jesus's actual birthdate. Most academics accept that if Christ was indeed born during the rule of Herod, then his birth must have been in 4 BC or earlier.

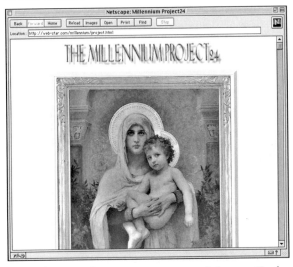

The seventeenth-century astronomer Johannes Kepler believed that Jesus was born seven years earlier because of cumulative errors made by Dionysus (see previous FAQ): not only did he fail to take into account the year zero, but Dionysus also omitted the four-year period when the Emperor Augustus was on the throne under the name Octavian (31–27 BC) and left out the first two years of his stepson Tiberius's rule after Augustus died. Kepler reckoned that this seven-year error tied in with the conjunction of Jupiter and Saturn in 7 BC, which St Matthew identified as the Star of Bethlehem.

But recently a leading Italian astronomer, Professor Giovanni Baratta, has claimed that Kepler also got it wrong, and that Jesus was born in 12 BC when an unusually bright 'travelling star' was observed between the constellations of Leo and Gemini. This comet was noted by Chinese as well as European astronomers at the time.

Depending on which theory is correct, the two-thousand-year anniversary of Jesus's birth could therefore have been in 1988, 1993, or 1996.

Why do we need calendars?

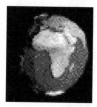 Calendars are essentially devices that adjust and regulate the differences between the natural divisions of time so that we can impose order on the astronomical clock of the universe. There are three basic cosmic sequences that define time – the rotation of the earth on its own axis, which defines the length of a 24-hour day; the rotation of the moon around the earth, which defines the lunar month; and the rotation of the earth around the sun, which defines a year. The other main sequence defining time is the week, but this is a purely artificial construct, based on the Biblical story of creation.

The first calendars are thought to have been invented by the Egyptians. They knew that the best time to plant their crops was immediately after the River Nile flooded each year, and the priests calculated that between each flooding the moon rose twelve times. They therefore counted twelve *moonths*, or months, and arrived at the first approximation of the length of a year.

The Egyptians also noticed that at floodtime each year a certain bright star would rise just before the sun did. They counted the days before this occurred again, and arrived at a figure of 365 days in the year. They then divided the year into twelve months of thirty days each, with five (sometimes six) extra days which became holy days.

How did leap years evolve?

Unfortunately, the natural cycles that define time are not easily divisible one into another. For instance, there are a variable number of days in the lunar month, and the number of days in the year don't add up to a round figure.

Despite this, the Egyptian calendar was eventually switched from a lunar one to one based on the rotation of the earth around the sun (365.25 days). But the extra quarter of a day in the solar calendar began to cause more and more confusion.

How was the problem of leap years resolved?

It was left to the Romans to sort out the confusion. Julius Caesar ordered that the year 46 BC should have 445 days to 'catch up', and that every fourth year from then on would have 366 days to use up the fractions left over from preceding years, thus introducing the concept of leap years.

The Julian calendar was in use up until the sixteenth century, but it then became apparent that too many 'extra' days were piling up and Easter and other holy days were not falling where they should. Easter, for example, was coming closer and closer to Christmas, the reason being that the true length of the cycle of the seasons (technically known as the tropical year) is 365.24219 days, not 365.25 days.

Pope Gregory's solution was to change the rules so that century years would only be leap years if they were divisible by 400. Effectively, this creates an adopted average of 365.2425 days in the year, an approximation that is within 30 seconds of the length of the tropical year and that the Royal Greenwich Observatory calculates will amount to a one-day error within 4000 years.

Italy adopted the Gregorian calendar in 1582, when ten days were 'dropped' from the year to make up the difference. Britain didn't adopt the calendar until 1752, by which time the margin of error was 11 days. During that particular year, September 2 was immediately followed by September 14.

Although various religions around the world maintain their own calendars for religious purposes, for everyday reckonings the Gregorian calendar is in use virtually world-wide.

Will 2000 be a leap year?

Yes. The rule is as follows:

"Every year that is exactly divisible by 4 is a leap year, except for years that are exactly divisible by 100. These centurial years are leap years only if they are divisible by 400. As a result, the year 2000 is a leap year, whereas 1900 and 2100 are not leap years."
The Explanatory Supplement to the Astronomical Almanac, 1992.

Why is there so much interest in the year 2000?

Ever since humanity became conscious of the fact just over a few hundred years ago that it was living 'in' a particular decade or century, people have tended to define their era by reference to groups of ten or a hundred years. We review a decade in terms of society's achievements and failures, natural disasters and other events, while at the same time looking forward to what might be on the horizon in the decade ahead. A century-long span offers an additional nuance, since it is at the upper limits of human life expectancy.

It is hardly surprising, therefore, that the year 2000 should carry with it some conceptual force, not to mention the weight of religious and millennial expectations. The magnetic pull it exerts is partly explained by the fact that it is the first time in history that so many people have shared the consciousness that a thousand-year time cycle is about to come to a close.

Even though cynics maintain that it is no more than a roll-over of digits on the clock, and party-poopers claim that the millennium doesn't start until 2001, the year 2000 has already generated a huge volume of features in the media, dozens of books on everything from millennial prophecies to the millennium time bomb, and hundreds of Web sites.

"The millennium is the comet that crosses the calendar every thousand years. It throws off metaphysical sparks. It promises a new age, or an apocalypse. It is a magic trick that time performs, extracting a millisecond from its eternal flatness and then, poised on that transitional instant, projecting a sort of hologram that teems with the summarised life of a thousand years just passed and with visions of the thousand now to come."
Time, Fall 1992.

What is a bimillennium?

A bimillennium is the anniversary of any event that took place 2000 years previously – a double millennium celebration. Strictly speaking, the anniversary of Christ's birth is a bimillennium celebration.

Where will the sun rise first on January 1, 2000?

The issue of where the sun will rise first has prompted a heated debate in the South Pacific between different contenders for the title. The difference between competing claims is only a matter of minutes (or, between some locations, mere seconds), but it is enough to separate winners from losers and to challenge the authenticity of rival millennium parties and television companies planning to sell their sunrise footage to the global networks.

Some 500 miles east of Christchurch in New Zealand, the Chatham Islands lie 155 miles from the dateline and are confident of their claim to be the first inhabited landmass to witness the millennium dawn. According to their calculations, the sun will rise over the 231m summit of Mount Hapeka on Pitt Island, the most easterly inhabited island in the group, at 3:59am (15:59 GMT) on the morning of January 1, 2000.

Television companies from Australia, Argentina, New Zealand, the United States and Britain are said to be competing for the film rights. The 750 islanders in the Chathams are anticipating a millennium invasion but with just one hotel, one lodge, one motel, one hostel and one flight a day from the mainland, tourist amenities are going to be stretched to the limit.

The Chathams' claim to the first sunrise was cast in doubt, however, by the decision of the tiny Pacific nation of Kiribati to 'move' the International Date Line in 1995, thus leap-frogging competitors to claim the first sunrise.

The International Date Line was drawn up at the International Meridian Conference in Washington, DC in 1884, at the same time that the world's 24 time zones were created. For most of its north-south journey through the Pacific the dateline follows the 180° meridian, but it zigzags around landmasses for obvious reasons – if it didn't do so, the inhabitants would find themselves living in different days of the week. Such was the case with Kiribati, with some islands ten hours behind GMT, others fourteen hours ahead.

On December 23, 1994, the Republic of Kiribati announced that: "with effect from January 1, 1995, all islands in the Line and Phoenix Groups shall be on the same day as the islands in the Gilberts Group within the Republic." This ruling created a huge, one-thousand-mile eastward loop in the dateline's course, shifting the easternmost islands from 'yesterday' to 'today'.

Several of Kiribati's islands are now in line for the first sunrise, notably Kiritimati (Christmas Island) and Caroline Island, which was renamed Millennium Island in 1997 in honour of this position.

But the change has not gone unchallenged by the other contenders. In November 1997 the *Geographical Journal*, published by the Royal Geographical Society, carried a weighty technical assessment of sunrise isochrons, declinations and complex equations to pinpoint the moment of sunrise. The paper concludes that "the Chatham Islands area of New Zealand, in particular certain hilltops on Pitt Island (also known as Rangiauria), will be the first inhabited places to see the first light on January 1, 2000 AD." It pours cold water on Kiribati's claims, by stating that the dateline change "lacks sensibility" and that the "arbitrary and unilateral moving of time zones or the International Date Line does not give rise to any level of credibility in the international navigation community."

The criticism displays a rather high-handed attitude towards the Kiribatians, for whom the change is eminently sensible. The Pitt Islanders, it might be noted, set their own time 45 minutes ahead of New Zealand for what they no doubt also consider valid reasons. More pertinently, the journal's findings (which have been widely reported in New Zealand) are open to accusations of commercial bias. One of the three co-authors is Norris McWhirter (founder of the *Guinness Book of Records*), whose Millennium Adventure Company has snapped up the rights (surprise, surprise) to film on certain hilltops on Pitt Island.

So who is right? The Old Royal Observatory at Greenwich comes down in favour of Pitt Island. "The international date-line has not been changed", says Maria Blyzinsky, astronomer at the Old Royal Observatory. "Although the time they're keeping in the Line and Phoenix Islands now puts them on the west side of the dateline, for scientific purposes they're not on the other side of the dateline and it won't be recognised by scientists or navigators."

"It all depends on which system you want to measure time by", says Blyzinsky. "The time zones system is a convenience which allows us to know roughly what time it is somewhere else in the world in comparison to ourselves, but it is just a social convention", she says. "The official system is Universal Time Coordinated (UTC), which is based on Greenwich Mean Time and the meridian, as determined by the Meridian Conference in Washington in 1884."

Confusingly, Dr Roger Catchpole of the Royal Greenwich Observatory in Cambridge believes that Kiribati's decision is legitimate. "There are good administrative reasons why Kiribati put all of its islands on the same day, and a not unre- alised consequence is that the Line Islands will be the first to see the local sunrise at the millennium. Our calculations show that it rises there at 15:43 GMT, and that Pitt Island will see it around 16:00 GMT."

So it's Millennium Island if you accept the dateline change, and Pitt Island if you don't. Considering the near-messianistic fervour currently being generated in Kiribati as the millennium approaches, it seems churlish to deny them their claim.

Sunrise times at the start of the year 2000

		GMT	LOCAL
Millennium Island, Kiribati	Dec 31, 1999	15:43	5:43
Flint Island, Kiribati	Dec 31, 1999	15:47	5:47
Antipodes Island	Dec 31, 1999	15:55	3:55
Pitt Island, NZ	Dec 31, 1999	16:00	4:45
Kiritimati, Kiribati	Dec 31, 1999	16:31	5:31
Mt Hikurangi, NZ	Dec 31, 1999	16:39	4:39
Katchall Island, Nicobar	Jan 1, 2000	00:00	6:00

Source: Royal Greenwich Observatory

Doesn't the New Year begin at midnight in Greenwich?

There is a twist in this tale of sunrise squabblings – they might all be wrong about where the new millennium actually begins. According to the International Meridian Conference, the universal day begins when it is 'mean midnight at the cross-hairs of the Airy transit circle in the Old Royal Observatory' at Greenwich. So the start of the new millennium is at 00:00 on January 1, 2000, measured in Universal Time. 'This would have to be regarded as the astronomical definition of the instant of the New Year', says the Royal Greenwich Observatory's Astronomy Research Council.

As the sunrise comes up over the Pacific, technically the New Year hasn't yet started since it is still around noon on

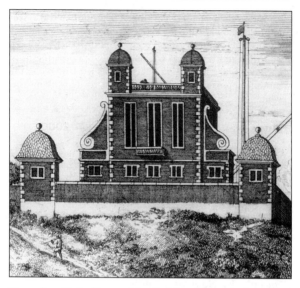

December 31 in Greenwich. And it will remain 'yesterday' until noon the following day.

This fact introduces a surprise contender into the global sunrise sweepstakes. When it is midnight on December 31 in Greenwich, where is the sun actually rising at that moment? The answer is in the Nicobar Islands, which lie within Indian territorial waters. "The sun is rising along half a great circle, across Russia, China and out over the Bay of Bengal, and at midnight GMT it will just be rising over an island called Katchall in the Nicobar group", says Dr Catchpole.

Located around 300km south of the Andaman Islands on the eastern side of the Bay of Bengal, the Nicobars are a restricted area with almost impossible access. A media race to film in the Nicobars seems unlikely, so perhaps the real first sunrise of the new millennium will shine down on Katchall, observed only by the dugongs, leatherback turtles and saltwater crocodiles who live around its shoreline – and maybe that's as it should be.

What is the curse of the countdown clocks?

Numerous millennium countdown clocks that claim to measure the time to midnight, December 31, 1999 to the nearest fraction of a second have been set up for public display in world capitals as well as on several Web sites. These clocks are all now incorrect.

The cause? It's called a leap second, and it is making a mockery of millennium clocks because of the differences in time as measured by atomic clocks and the rotation of the earth.

Is the atomic clock accurate?

First demonstrated by the National Physical Laboratory at Teddington, England, in 1995, the atomic clock superseded all previous methods of timekeeping by virtue of its astonishing accuracy enabling it to keep time to one second within 300 years. The caesium atoms that control this accuracy are not stationary, however, and tiny errors arise when their frequency is altered. In addition, the earth itself is a relatively poor timekeeper, since the varying effects of the oceans and molten core on its spin rate cause the planet to slow down or speed up fractionally year by year.

As a result, the time according to atomic clocks gets gradually out of synchronisation with the time as measured by the rotation of the planet – the latter is known as Universal Time (UT) and is for all intents and purposes the same as Greenwich Mean Time (GMT).

The solution is leap seconds, which are inserted every now and then into atomic time to create Universal Time Coordinated (UTC).

How do these complications affect countdown clocks?

First, if you go to Greenwich and have the time printed out on your commemorative ticket, what it actually shows you is the atomic time (UTC) and not GMT as they would have you believe. Second, there are likely to be several more leap seconds introduced into atomic clocks before the millennium (they were last recalibrated for an extra second in June 1997). This might not appear to matter too much, but in fact the anomaly means that it is impossible to know how many more seconds will elapse before millions of people raise their glasses for a toast at midnight on December 31, 1999.

"The millennium is freighted with immense historical symbolism and psychological power. It does not depend on objective calculation, but entirely on what people bring to it – their hopes, their anxieties, the metaphysical focus of their attention. The millennium is essentially an event of the imagination."
Time, Fall 1992.

What is the millennium time bomb?

Also known as the Y2K (Year 2000) problem, or simply the millennium bomb, it refers to the fact that computers all over the world may crash as their date systems roll 1999 over into 2000.

The problem originates with the design of early computer programmes, when memory was at such a premium that programmers shortened commands to a minimum whenever they could. This included shortening the year to just two numbers (ie '56' instead of 1956) so that the date came to be represented as DD/MM/YY (08/03/56, for example). Although this seems like a tiny saving, dates occur so often in

The millennium apocalypse

Computer chaos
BUSI

Business 'too late to avoid havoc in 2000'

'Act now or face train chaos for year 2000'

THE RAIL industry was being warned   by DICK MURRAY   smaller firms, th all electronic retro

meltdown

Millennium bug 'poses threat to nuclear sector'

software systems that it saved memory space many times over, and programmers had no idea that these original computer languages would still be operating at the end of the century.

With the development of more powerful computers, the logic for this abbreviation has long since disappeared, but meanwhile it had become standard convention throughout the programming world.

As 1999 clicks over into 2000 the computer will register only '00', recognising the year as 1900 rather than 2000. It may then become confused, believe it has been tampered with, and shut down altogether. British tourists to the US have been aware of this anomaly for over a decade, since their driving licenses, which have expiry dates well into the next century, were being rejected by the computer systems of car rental companies.

Experts warn of disruption on a worldwide scale, as everything from cash dispensers to air traffic control systems and elevators begins to malfunction. Almost everything containing a microchip could be at risk. Some people predict that as dawn breaks over the Pacific and spreads across the globe, up to 50,000 mainframes will crash in succession, causing a wave of economic, political and social chaos that will engulf the entire world.

The nightmare scenario could well result in a situation where databases that normally calculate taxes, pensions, mortgages and utility bills suddenly begin to churn out rubbish. Children might be sent pensions and pensioners might automatically be added to primary school intake lists; a hundred years of interest could be added to savings accounts, or vice versa, with massive amounts in interest debited to credit cards or bank balances. Everything from military hardware to civilian aircraft may be simultaneously scheduled for maintenance.

On the home front, 'slave' chips that control domestic appliances could go similarly awry. You might wake up with a hangover on January 1, 2000 to find the burglar alarm going off, the refrigerator defrosting, the boiler shut down, and the video and microwave simply failing to function. Don't think you can escape chaos by leaping in your car and driving away. If it has a chip controlling its engine, it won't start. You won't be able to catch the train either, since computers that control key safety systems such as signalling and power supplies would have shut down.

Every single computer in existence has an embedded clock, and most software features a mathematical representation of the date. On January 1, 2000, the two-digit format ceases to function. This is what amounts to the millennium time bomb.

It has already been called the biggest human-made disaster to hit the information technology industry. It is, in fact, a wonderfully appropriate and ironic apocalyptic scenario for millennial expectations in the age of the computer.

Things that might go haywire on January 1, 2000

Air conditioners, airplanes, air traffic control systems, automatic doors, bar code readers, cafeteria equipment, cameras, cars, cash registers, clocks, credit card scanners, electronic vaults, emergency lighting, escalators, fax machines, fire alarms, fridge/freezers, heating systems, helicopters, hospital equipment, lifts, lighting systems, medical equipment, microwaves, military hardware, missile systems, motorised wheelchairs, optical readers, pagers, photocopiers, postage meters, power management systems, printers, satellite receivers, scanners, security gates, telephones, thermostats, time clocks, traffic lights, vending machines, video recorders, water heaters.

Will the millennium time bomb really go off?

Banking and insurance are the industries most likely to be thrown into chaos, but they are probably least at risk since they have been aware of the problem for a long time, and most have already worked out solutions.

Unfortunately, any solution involves enormous costs, since an average business may have several million lines of code in their computer systems and each line has to be checked. Even though systems have been developed which do this automatically (the so-called 'magic bullet' solution), they aren't necessarily foolproof and the only way to be sure is to check each line of code manually to make sure no obscure date codes are missed. There are also millions of chips embedded in locations where removal and testing becomes a major technical operation.

How expensive is this time bomb?

In Britain alone, the cost of reprogramming computers has been put at £52 billion (US$83b), although even that may be a conservative estimate, with the total cost of altering government programmes estimated at £12 billion (US$19b) alone.

Taskforce 2000, the British government agency set up to deal with the millennium time bomb, says that 80-90 percent of all computer systems will need to be changed and that many companies are burying their heads in the sand.

In the US, it's estimated that 300 to 600 billion lines of code will have to be analysed, and either rewritten or discarded.

Worldwide the cost is estimated at £370 billion (US$592b), a figure that represents the total cost of the Vietnam War and the Kobe earthquake combined.

Even if a company does manage to sort out its own systems, it could still be affected if its customers and suppliers don't do the same. If external systems aren't 'clean', they could infect the host computer. Some consultants estimate that up to five percent of all businesses will go bust if testing is not completed in time.

Given that even in regions with well-developed computer industries (such as the US, the Far East and Europe) awareness of the time bomb and efforts to defuse it in time are behind schedule, the situation in other countries approaches the unthinkable. The magazine *Information Week* has estimated that 50 percent of businesses worldwide will not be converted in time for the millennium.

The Bank Vault Problem

The microchip that controls a twenty-tonne bank vault door is buried inside the door for security reasons and it only allows the door to be opened from Monday to Friday, not on weekends. The bank building itself has been built around the door, again for security reasons. No one could have foreseen that the chip might need to be changed. As January 1, 2000 (which is a Saturday) rolls around, the chip will think it is January 1, 1900, which was a Monday. So the door will be open all weekend, but it will close on Wednesday night, January 5, 2000. A problem for the bank – for which there is only one solution in order to get at the chip, and that is to actually demolish the building.

Is there a positive side to the millennium time bomb?

Only if you are a computer programmer. It's thought that in Britain alone at least 300,000 staff will be needed to fix the problem, the equivalent of all the computer professionals in the country. In 1998 the computer giant ICL not only started recruiting retired pensioners, but also entered into talks with the Prisons Service to employ inmates to help rewrite billions of lines of code. Cobol programming skills are already in great demand, and likely to become more so. As the immutable deadline of 2000 approaches and businesses start to wake up to the problem, consultancy fees are set to escalate. Computer companies are already making plans for rescuing 'non-compliant' systems as the millennium dawns, reportedly forecasting fees of up to £1000 (US$1630) a day. The computer services group Logica claims that it would have cost a medium-sized company £1.5 million (US$2.4m) to update their systems in 1997, but by 1998, the bill will have risen to £3.3 million (US$5.4m).

Lawyers will also be happy with their lot. Businesses that don't solve their millennium bugs can expect lawsuits from shareholders, clients and customers. The American consultancy firm Gartner estimates that the legal costs could amount to a staggering US$1 trillion (£613b).

According to a report in the London newspaper *The Guardian* in January 1997, the major spring clean of software systems now going on has had another unexpected side-effect. Programmers may start uncovering overcharging and underpayments for rent, taxation, music and publishing royalties, interest, dividends and insurance premiums which could date back decades. Whether anyone will inform the recipients of their unexpected windfalls is another matter.

What about the 2000 leap year?

Quite. Even ordinary leap years can often catch out software systems. On December 30, 1996, aluminium smelters in New Zealand and Tasmania shut down when the computers decided they couldn't make sense of the unexpected 366th day of the year. The total bill was £1 million (US$1.63m). The real complication this time for the computers is that 2000 is the exception to the exception, when the extra day is put back in. Further chaos is almost certain to follow.

Will the millennium time bomb affect my computer?

For IBM-compatible PC users, 32-bit Windows applications (Windows 95 and NT) can deal with dates up to 2099. But 16-bit Windows programmes are not millennium-proof. To test your system, set the time and date to 11.58 on December 31, 1999, exit Windows and turn off the computer. Wait a few minutes, re-boot and check what time and date it displays. It is estimated that four out of five PCs will revert to either 1980 or 1984 on January 1, 2000.

Even once this is sorted out, further problems will arise with Windows-compatible software. Early releases of spreadsheet programmes such as Lotus 1-2-3, Excel and Quattro Pro are not millennium-compliant. Apple Mac operating systems will apparently not be affected, although there may be problems with applications that use dates.

> *"A millennial year has occurred only once before: fifty generations ago, in the year 1000, on what was a very different, more primitive planet earth. So this one has a strange, cosmic prestige, a quality almost of the unprecedented. The world approaches it in states of giddiness, expectation and, consciously or unconsciously, a certain anxiety."*
>
> *Time*, Fall 1992.

What is *fin de siècle malaise*, and is it catching?

The phrase *fin de siècle* ('end of century') was first used in France in 1885, and was soon taken up as the title for a novel by Emile Zola and also a play which was performed in Paris in 1888. By the 1890s the term was in widespread use in English-speaking countries, indeed to such an extent that one august journal complained in 1891 that "everywhere we are treated to dissertations on *fin-de-siècle* literature, *fin-de-siècle* statesmanship, *fin-de-siècle* morality".

'*Fin de siècle malaise*' (literally 'end of century disquiet') may have had its origins in the writer Chateaubriand's earlier use of the phrase *mal de siècle* but passed into the vernacular as a term describing a general sense of fatigue, self-doubt, disenchantment and weariness as the nineteenth century neared its end.

A similar sense of overwhelming morbidity is echoed today in the predictions of environmentalists, millenarian groups and Doomsday cults, but *fin de siècle malaise* is unlikely to

Mad cow scientist warns of plague in 2000

'I've tried normal ways and you end up with government and financial interests lying. Fiction may well be a better vehicle for my claims', says Dr Lacey, left. Rabies and its spread, as seen above in a Central Office of Information film, and aphids are two of the protagonists in his novel *Red, Yellow and Blue make White.*

Main photograph: Science Photo Library

become a fashionable complaint at the end of the twentieth century. Instead, you are much more likely to succumb to less dramatic anxieties – whether or not, for instance, you have been invited to the best and biggest New Year's Eve party.

What is premillennial angst?

A more modern and intense manifestation of *fin de siècle malaise* is the experience of premillennial angst – an acute sense of foreboding and heightened expectation relating to the arrival of the Millennium and/or the Second Coming. Most likely to apply to Doomsday groups, evangelical churches, UFO enthusiasts and other millennial cults, premillennial angst also manifests itself in a general feeling of unease about 'endings'. Dwelling on personal or global cataclysms, experiencing a sense of hopelessness in the face of overwhelming events – in a millennial context, this is premillennial angst.

What is premillennial tension?

Premillennial tension is the name given to outbreaks of hysterical behaviour amongst members of evangelical groups in anticipation of the Rapture to follow in the year 2000. The Toronto Blessing, for instance, has been described as a classic incidence of premillennial tension. In 1994 thousands of worshippers at a small church near Toronto were overcome with 'Holy Spirit Fever' during services, which caused them to fall over, laughing uncontrollably, or to lie perfectly still with beatific smiles on their faces. The phenomenon also spread to England, where it was given the name Premillennial Tension, or PMT (pun intended), by Dr Andrew Walker of King's College, London. Premillennial tension also has a secular meaning, since it has become a fashionable label for any manifestation of contemporary culture with a vaguely apocalyptic theme.

"Familiar elements of trendy, pre-millennium Zeitgeist fever abound, as everything bar the kitchen sink is thrown into a great big digital melting pot, simmering slowly until it erupts into a full-on club experience meltdown."
Neil Cooper reviewing Nacionale Vite Activa, *The Times*, April 9, 1997.

What is millenarianism?

Millenarianism is a term that can be applied to any set of beliefs which envisage imminent salvation. In his classic work *The Pursuit of the Millennium*, Norman Cohn defines millenarian sects as those which picture salvation to be collective (the faithful will be saved), terrestrial (it takes place on earth rather than in heaven), imminent (it will come both soon and suddenly), total (life will be completely transformed), and miraculous (supernatural agencies will be involved). Within these parameters there is still enormous scope for imagining how the millennium is going to happen and the route to reaching it.

Over the centuries the millennial myth has surfaced in countries and cultures all over the world, from medieval Europe to eighteenth-century China and from Melanesia to twentieth-century America. Its broad sweep has led to the accommodation of beliefs as diverse as those of survivalists, Raëlians, UFO freaks, conspiracy theorists, utopians, and a whole bevy of latter-day prophets. The New Age movement has powerful millennial resonances, as does the environmental movement.

What is chiliasm?

Chilias, derived from the Greek *khilioi* meaning 'thousand', is an alternative word for millenarianism. Its main use to date has been by millenarian scholars.

What on earth (or in heaven) is meant by premillennial, amillennial and postmillennial beliefs?

The cryptic language in which the Book of Revelation is written does not allow for a single, unambiguous interpretation of the text. Christian scholars, amongst others, have been debating its precise meaning for centuries and are continuing to do so today. Essentially, the premillennialists believe that the millennial party can't get going until humankind has been redeemed through the Second Coming of Christ; the postmillennialists believe that the party has already started; and the amillennialists think that there isn't going to be a party after all.

According to the premillennialists, the Second Coming will be preceded by signs such as wars, famine, earthquakes and other tribulations, along with the appearance of the

Antichrist. Christ will then descend, vanquish the Antichrist at the battle of Armageddon, and reign over a millennium of peace and righteousness. During this Golden Age dead believers will be raised and will mingle with the rest of the world's inhabitants (in their 'glorified bodies'), and at the end of the millennium the rest of the (non-Christian) dead will be raised, and the world divided into the eternal states of heaven and hell.

By contrast, the postmillennialists believe that Christ already reigns through his church on earth, and that when Christianity is eventually accepted throughout the world, Christ will return to rule for a thousand years of spiritual harmony.

Amillennialists do not believe in the literal truth of Revelation, or in the thousand-year reign of Christ. For them, the millennium of Revelation is a description of the kingdom of heaven where Christ already rules over deceased believers.

What are the chances of apocalypse in the year 2000?

The chances are fairly high if you're thinking in terms of asteroid impacts and the destruction of the planet. At a conference of the Geological Society in London in February 1997, scientists claimed that our planet is long over- due a collision with an asteroid or comet that would cause widespread devasta- tion similar to that which led to the extinction of the dinosaurs 65 million years ago. Such an impact, thousands of times more powerful than the Hiroshima bomb, would send up a cloud of debris which would blot out the sun and send global temperatures plummeting. It would probably kill

around a quarter of the world's population. It might happen in 2000, but there again, it might not happen until 3000.

There is also the possibility of a wide variety of Doomsday scenarios involving the millennium time bomb. If, for instance, it precipitated a wave of computer crashes, the possibility of worldwide economic meltdown followed by panic, rioting and the collapse of social order always exists. If it coincided with a global telecommunications breakdown, things might be even worse. In October 1997 a power failure in just one satellite led to the collapse of the Indian telecommunications system, closing down the stock market and affecting telephone, television, the rail system and essential government services for a week. How many satellites are year 2000-compliant?

Missile systems and other armaments are a further sensitive area. In the UK the Ministry of Defence has spent £100 million (US$163m) on reprogramming its weapons systems and, no doubt, other advanced industrialised countries have followed suit. But what of the nuclear missiles in the former Soviet republics, or the military arsenals in Iraq, Iran, Libya, China, and elsewhere? Has anyone *told* these countries that they've got to reset the clocks on their bombs and missiles?

Nuclear power plants are another hot issue. It's reported that British plants may have to be temporarily shut down in case of sudden malfunction, at a time, incidentally, when there will be peak electricity demand from millions of people partying through the night. Has anyone bothered to share this information with Argentina, South Africa, Bulgaria, Romania, the Philippines, Mexico, Cuba, Pakistan, Turkey, Brazil, Switzerland, Sweden, France, Iran, Hungary, Poland, Spain, the Russian republics, Austria, the Czech Republic and Slovakia, India, Korea or Taiwan?

Nature's Doomsday contribution is the predicted increase in sunspot activity in the year 2000. Sunspots follow an eleven-year cycle, and the last major eruption was in 1989. Sunspots cause what are known as 'coronal mass ejections', also called sunstorms, whereby clouds of burning hot plasma stream out from the sun at speeds of up to two million miles per hour, buffeting the earth's magnetic field and generating huge amounts of electricity with the capacity to knock out entire national grids and disable satellites. In 1989 eight million homes in Canada lost power and two crucial communications satellites malfunctioned as a result of sunstorms. The storms predicted for 2000 could have catastrophic consequences.

Apocalyptic theorists will no doubt have a field day with the revelation that the US military's space tracking systems are rendered completely blind during sunstorms. Their purpose is to make sure that satellites falling to earth are not mistaken for incoming ICBMs (intercontinental ballistic missiles), but during sunstorms not only do their monitoring systems break down but also many satellites or items of space debris experience increased drag and are more likely to crash out of the skies. A sunstorm is the perfect cover for any sufficiently alert dictator to launch a nuclear attack, and in the year 2000 there may well be many such opportunities.

So we might wake up to more than just a hangover on January 1, 2000?

Imagine the scenario. At one minute past midnight everyone is boozily cheering in the new millennium when all of a sudden things start to go wrong in a big way. A nuclear power plant goes on red alert near a major capital in Asia, inducing widespread panic. Computers start to go down across the Pacific, knocking out air traffic control on busy sectors. Inevitably, there is a horrific crash, perhaps involving two or more planes on the approach to an airport. An ICBM in a silo somewhere in Uzbekhistan suddenly decides it's past its sell-by-date and launches itself towards Chicago. The US manages to intercept it with an antiballistic missile somewhere over Newfoundland, but the resulting fall-out spreads radioactive dust across half of Canada.

A burst of sunstorm activity knocks out many more satellites, plunging communications into chaos, and a Middle East

Millennium's Eve Parties
The International Register

This register of places to party on New Year's Eve 2000 and 2001 has been set up so that everybody who wants to party somewhere on those momentous evenings can choose from a list of venues.

For a discussion of the correct time to celebrate the coming of the new millennium, we suggest that you consult this document. If you are any the wiser afterwards, please let us know when your party will be!

So make your plans now for the big event. Early booking is recommended to avoid disappointment. Our lists already feature a variety of celebrations, in places all round the globe.

If you are running a club, pub, or street party, or simply want crowds of gate-crashers at your private party, add your venue to this list. If in doubt, please ask a responsible person first.

Listings can be added and will appear immediately on-line in the recent additions category, and at regular intervals the recent additions will be categorised into various sections.

In association with Epage we bring you a classified ad service for party supplies. Millennium party planners - check these pages for the goods and services you require.

---

dictator decides to take advantage of the military blackout to launch a missile attack on Israel. Israel retaliates.

The giant video screens relaying global parties in public squares suddenly go blank, and televisions worldwide 'go to noise'. The Internet (designed to be war-proof) survives and, as rumours of worldwide chaos spread like wildfire, millions panic.

Looting and rioting breaks out in major cities. Hordes of people flee the cities, forming vast roving bands that terrorise the countryside. Governments retreat to their bunkers as the army steps in to restore order. Prophets and apocalyptic soothsayers appear amidst the masses, hailing the arrival of the Second Coming. Thousands camp out in the deserts of New Mexico and California, anticipating the descent of star fleets who are to save the world, or the descent of the 'Elohim'. Churches get their best congregations ever, as millions pray for salvation.

The millennium certainly could be one helluva party!

Who will do well out of the Millennium?

Airlines (expecting the busiest year in aviation history); big-name bands and rock stars; champagne producers and importers; computer programmers and software companies offering millennium time bomb solutions; construction workers and engineers, particularly in Sydney, Hannover and London; corporate lawyers; costume rental shops; cruise ship companies; fireworks manufacturers and pyrotechnic display artists; hotels all over the world (particularly luxury hotels); the pope (papal souvenirs, ranging from Holy Year 2000 key-rings to Holy Year 2000 commemorative medals are already being sold on the Internet); property developers in Greenwich and Docklands; property owners in Sydney (rentals are expected to go up by around 250 percent); tour operators; waiters and waitresses (catering companies in 1997 were offering contracts paying £50 an hour for New Year's Eve 1999).

Is there any copyright on the word 'millennium'?

As the year 2000 approaches the world is about to overdose on millennium hype, with hundreds of products and services bearing the 'millennium' label. Information technology companies were amongst the first to jump on the bandwagon, either because they wanted to project a futuristic image or because they were involved in solving millennium time bomb problems. But now the marketing frenzy has reached absurd proportions. The US Patent and Trademark Office has already awarded 117 trademarks that include 'millennium' and more than 1500 with '2000' in the title, and thousands more are pending.

In Britain hundreds of companies have registered similar trademarks. Curiously, the first registration was made nearly a century ago: an application by the Royal Botanic Gardens at Kew to use 'millennium' for seeds and plants was made in 1902.

Few of the products being marketed bear any relation to the millennium. In the US, millennium merchandise includes chocolates, champagne, beer, floor wax, golf balls, motor oil, power saw blades, pest control products, gas masks, under-wear, vacuum cleaners, electric light fixtures, and even wind chimes.

In Britain you can already buy the Millennium Kettle and fairly soon there'll be Millennium Ale, a Millennium Chair, Millennium Marmalade, Millennium Jewellery, and Next Millennium Kitchens. An environmentally friendly fuel treat-ment 'for the next century' almost justifies the millennium tag and a Millennium Cocktail sounds like a winner, but what of millennium car tyres, industrial lubricants, fishing tackle, beds, electric showers, herbicides, tea, bicycles, and artificial limbs?

Britain's Design Council has also jumped on board with a campaign to promote 2000 'Millennium Products', the top 200 of which will be on display at the millennium exhibition. A British supermarket chain unveiled a £4 million (US$6.5m) programme to upgrade its trolleys in 1997, claiming that they had designed 'the trolley for the millennium'. *Playboy* wants to be the 'Official Magazine of the Millennium', and Britain's *Daily Mirror* carried the masthead slogan 'The Newspaper for the Millennium' briefly during 1997.

But the generic branding of the millennium has other implications. A New York company, Planet Marketing, holds the rights to use 'Year 2000' on clothing, footwear and novelties, and even has a full-time worker searching the Internet for anyone who might have the temerity to attempt to use the slogan. A computer analyst from Maine, David Bettinger, discovered this to his cost when he started selling 'Year 2000' T-shirts and found himself on the receiving end of a cease-and-desist letter from the company's lawyers. "I was astounded that they could even get a trademark on that term", Bettinger told the Associated Press. "It irks me that I can be receiving so much heat from people who are representing this generic term. How ludicrous is that?"

Not as ludicrous, perhaps, as some of the attempts to hijack the event by millennium party planners. The Washington-based Millennium Society tried to lobby Congress in June 1997 to approve a bill that would have made it the official body overseeing all activities in the United States connected with the millennium. The bill called for the organisation to receive trademark rights and funding through commemorative US coins and postage stamps, reported the *Star Tribune*, but the legislation was defeated when lobbyists from competing millennial entrepreneurs rallied against it.

" 'Millennium' is a name already widely used by businesses. It makes sense, then, that in 1999–2001 this will be extended to bouncing millennium babies... More than just a soothing, sonorous word, 'Millennium' implies longevity, remembrance and legacy – virtues which are perennially popular with parents choosing names", explains Mildred Felch of the British Name Federation. " 'Millennium' is strong, male and shortens well to 'Mills', while 'Millennia' is delicate, feminine, and can of course be shortened to 'Millie'."

From Shift Control

Ⓦ http://www.shiftcontrol.com/archive/timeshift/mill-name24.html

Is it possible to celebrate the millennium more than once?

Indeed it is, by the simple expedient of celebrating New Year's Eve in a country to the west of the International Date Line, and then catching a flight on January 1, 2000 eastwards, thereby losing a day and arriving in time to celebrate New Year's Eve all over again.

Some airlines are reported to be planning not to fly their planes as the millennium dawns, however, because of doubts about air traffic control and navigation systems. But 80 percent of the world's aircraft are airborne at any moment in time, and there simply wouldn't be enough space at the world's airports if they all had to stay on the ground.

Popular party destinations for two-timing travellers are likely to include Tonga, Kiribati, Sydney, Melbourne, Auckland, Fiji, and Tokyo for the first night, and Samoa, the Cook Islands, Tahiti or the US for the second night. Several tour operators are already offering packages of this nature, with parties at top hotels thrown in. Flights across the Pacific on January 1 are likely to become heavily booked. Start planning now if you want to join the mile-high hangover club.

In fact, plenty of people will be celebrating the millennium twice anyway, because there will be celebrations on New Year's Eve 2000 (the start of the real millennium) as well as on New Year's Eve 1999.

Can Concorde beat the clock?

Theoretically, yes. You could celebrate the passing of midnight three times on a transatlantic Concorde trip: once in London, once in mid-air, and once in New York. But because you would have to take off just after midnight in London to arrive in New York just before midnight, the first midnight party would probably have to be held in a hangar at

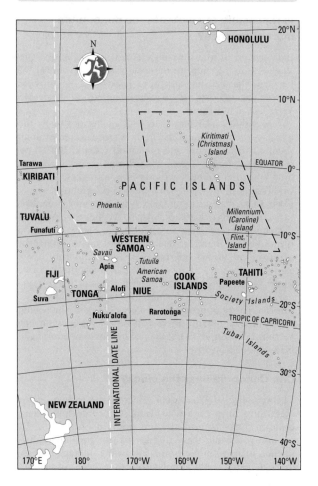

Heathrow, and the second somewhere within the airport in New York. But there are other problems to overcome – both airports are usually closed at that time anyway, and they're unlikely to want to open up simply to accommodate a bunch of high-flying party-goers.

British Airways say they have been inundated with requests from individuals, corporations and other groups who want to charter their planes. "We've got seven Concordes to play with, and an entire working group trying to figure out what the possibilities are", said a spokesman. The charters may be auctioned off for charity. An announcement on where BA's seven Concordes will be flying on New Year's Eve 1999 was expected to have been made in Spring 1998 after we went to press.

In the Pacific, there is the possibility that one or more Concordes will take off after dawn on January 1, 2000 from places to the west of the dateline such as Kiritimati (Christmas Island) in Kiribati, which has a massive airstrip, or Sydney, and fly to the United States, where it will still be December 31, 1999.

Where can I go to avoid the millennium?

You could try taking an extended holiday in China, where it will be the year 4698, although the Chinese have already dispatched TV crews to New Zealand to film the millennium preparations, so perhaps you might not be able to escape it in China after all.

Any Islamic country is probably a safe bet (in the Islamic calendar it will be the year 1420), as are remote areas of India and Asia. Large tracts of Africa and South America will be completely unaffected by the millennium, apart from areas with Catholic populations.

Forget about seeking sanctuary on a mountain top; every peak with spiritual connotations (and to some people, that's any peak at all) will probably be verging on the overcrowded.

Fundamentalist Christians are already being urged to make their way to the mountain tops to await the Second Coming, and New Age believers hold that the only way to survive the forthcoming changes is to live in the mountains and prepare for the Dawning of the Age of Aquarius.

At the world's special landmarks – the Taj Mahal, Machu Picchu, and so on, it's likely to be a bit of a crush.

Can't I stay at home and ignore the millennium?

Not easily if you are a computer user, since if you ignore it, your software programmes will probably crash.

It will also be impossible to avoid in the global media. During the course of 1999, television, radio and print media will be awash with retrospective histories of civilisation and human achievements over the last 100, 1000 or 2000 years, along with countless lists detailing 'the best of' almost everything covering two millennia. Millennial cults, prophecies and apocalyptic expectations will also come under the media spotlight. Numerous programmes and features will appear looking ahead to the next 1000 years, with pundits speculating on the future shape of world affairs, science and technology.

On New Year's Eve 1999 most television channels will be screening their own versions of the celebrations taking place around the world, with 24-hour telecasts linking all the big parties in different time zones. Stirring messages from world political and religious leaders will run alongside fundraising events and human interest stories – the camera crews will probably swamp maternity wards and stand there with stopwatches waiting for the first 'millennium babies' to be born.

Who won't be celebrating the millennium?

Around 3.8 billion people, or the two-thirds of the world who live in predominantly non-Christian countries. That still leaves nearly two billion people who will be observing it in some form or other (even if only to dip into the worldwide telecasts on New Year's Eve 1999), making it the biggest mass celebration in the history of humanity. Other people who won't be celebrating the millennium are those staffing crisis helplines. Suicides run at record levels on New Year's Eve, and 1999 is expected to be a particularly bad year.

Where is the safest place to be on January 1, 2000?

Probably in the middle of a field, a long way from airports, army bases, power plants, motorways, cities and computers.

THE MILLENNIUM

GUIDE

AUSTRALIA

Australia is preparing for a massive influx during the year 2000 as between 100,000 and 200,000 spectators, athletes, officials and journalists descend on **Sydney** for the Olympic Games. The city is also gearing up for a mega New Year's Eve party on December 31, 1999, although one person who won't be joining in is Prime Minister John Howard. Answering a parliamentary question on the subject, he stated that "both the twenty-first century and the third millennium will begin on Monday, 1 January, 2001", and festivities would therefore coincide with the Centenary of Federation on January 1, 2001. Technically he is right (see FAQs), but the statement shocked the hedonistic Aussies, who were looking forward to the biggest booze-up of the century.

The rest of the world is celebrating 2000 despite this, so it looks like the Aussies are going to have a party a year too late – or at least the prime minister will be the only one to miss the festivities on New Year's Eve 1999.

Aside from the Olympics, other events taking place include **Planet Earth 2000**, a world horticultural festival, and a major Green parties conference, **Greens Global 2001**.

Sydney

Sydney is busy preparing for the **Olympics 2000** with a building bonanza, as up to AUS$10 million (£4m/US$6.6m) a day is spent on construction projects in the lead-up to the opening ceremonies. But the Olympics are embroiled in numerous controversies, including overpaid executives, a polluted site,

and the prospect of being left with a white elephant once the Olympic Stadium is completed – problems that are remarkably similar to those surrounding the Millennium Dome in Greenwich, London.

Sydney is ready to party, however, and began the warm-up back in 1996, with a stunning fireworks display stretching across the entire harbour, launched from 25 different locations including Sydney Harbour Bridge itself. A team of seventy pyrotechnicians launched over 16,000 fireworks containing over five tonnes of explosives, the whole show choreographed against a backdrop of flame-lit barges with timpani drummers and a 'boat ballet' set to symphony music. The city is planning a variety of experimental themes in the coming years, 'testing different ideas and concepts so that the year 2000 is a spectacular no one can beat'.

Olympic Games 2000

Opening ceremony: September 15, 2000

After the traditional flame-lighting ceremony in Greece, the Olympic torch will be flown to Australia, where torch-bearers will continue the relay around the country, ending in the Olympic Stadium on September 15, 2000, when the Olympic Flame cauldron will be lit, signalling the start of the Games.

The Games: September 16–October 1, 2000

More than 10,000 athletes from 171 nations are expected to compete in the Games of the XXVII Olympiad being held in Sydney. The Games will take place in two zones – in the Harbour Zone and in the Sydney Olympic Park, situated at Homebush Bay 14km from the city centre, which will include the 110,000-seater Olympic Stadium. All athletes will live in the one Olympic Village, within walking distance of the main stadium.

Sydney Organising Committee for the Olympic Games (SOCOG), PO Box 2000, Sydney NSW 2001 Ⓣ 02/9297 2000 Ⓕ 9297 2020
Ⓦ http://www.sydney.olympic.org
Comprehensive and well-organised pages detailing every single aspect of the Sydney 2000 Olympics.

Paralympic Games: October 18–29, 2000

The Paralympic Games will be the largest staged since the first one was held in 1960, with over 4000 athletes taking part in eighteen sports (fourteen of which are Olympic sports).

Sydney Paralympic Organising Committee (SPOC), PO Box R383, Royal Exchange, Sydney NSW 2000 Ⓣ 02/9297 2000 Ⓕ 9297 2355.

Olympic Arts Festival

The Olympic Arts Festival is a four-year programme of cultural events which kicked off with 1997's highly successful

Festival of the Dreaming, celebrating the world's indigenous cultures.

A Sea Change: September 15–October 5, 1998

This event focuses on historic global movements of exploration and settlement, commemorating immigrants, explorers, or fugitives from war and suffering.

Reaching the World: Throughout 1999

A touring festival with the best of Australia's creative artists and performers will visit countries throughout the world.

Harbour of Life: June 23–October 29, 2000

This four-month programme will feature a great festival of nations and new works, performances and exhibitions by leading international and creative artists.

Greens Global 2001

Newcastle, NSW: Easter, 2001

Greens Global 2001 is an initiative to bring together Green parties from all over the world, but particularly from the Asia-Pacific region, in order to devise strategies for tackling the problems of the next millennium and build on the international strengths of the Green movement.

Deb Foskey, International Secretary, Australian Greens, c/o Dept of Political Science, ANU, Canberra, ACT 0200 ☏ 02/6281 0873 🅕 6249 5054
🅔 Deborah.Foskey@anu.edu.au 🅦 http://www.peg.apc.org/~ausgreen/

Mt Penang, Gosford, New South Wales: Planet Earth 2000

August 2000–January 2001

The first International Garden Festival to be held in the southern hemisphere, and only the third to be held outside Europe,

Ocean Rescue 2000

Launched in 1991, Ocean Rescue 2000 is a ten-year programme aimed at strengthening and extending Australia's existing conservation policies to ensure sustainable use of marine resources into the next millennium. Although Australia's Great Barrier Reef Marine Park has always been considered a model for marine conservation elsewhere in the world, the country's marine environment is actually under threat from numerous sources, including overfishing, toxic run-off from agricultural and industrial activities, and habitat destruction. Some of its famous surfing beaches are contaminated by domestic sewage, and litter has created a health hazard on many others. Backed by the Commonwealth Government, Ocean Rescue 2000's aim is to guarantee a sustainable future for Australia's coastal waters, which extend for almost nine million square kilometres – an area 16 percent larger than the country itself.

Planet Earth 2000 is expected to attract around five million people to its 58-hectare site at Mt Penang, on the New South Wales central coast. During the six months of the festival, over twenty million plants will be on display, with themed gardens created by over forty participating countries. Specialist glasshouse and aviary environments, tropical, wetlands and rainforest areas will exhibit Australia's unique flora and fauna. Planet Earth 2000 is also expected to be a showcase for innovative technology in horticulture and has a strong environmental theme. The AUS$237 million (£91m/ US$148m) festival is being backed by the Commonwealth and New South Wales governments and will also feature cultural events and entertainment, Aboriginal dance, art and 'bush tucker', classical and jazz music festivals, and street theatre. The site, overlooking Brisbane Water, is surrounded by National Park and the inten-

Olympics 2000 – Behind the Razzmatazz

Sydney's carefully orchestrated campaign to host the Olympics ensured that the city narrowly beat Beijing at the finish line, but since then the Australian press has given the Committee for Sydney's Olympic Games (SOCOG) a hard ride over issues such as the undisclosed salaries paid to Olympic officials, the huge cost of the Olympic stadium itself, and the fate of the stadium after the Games have finished. Members of Parliament were also in revolt over the high cost of the Games, which by the summer of 1997 were revealed to be around AUS$5.2 billion (£2b/US$3.4b). Further problems loomed as the International Olympic Committee warned that Sydney's transport infrastructure would be strained to capacity and that hotel accommodation would be in short supply.

But the biggest controversy surrounds revelations by Greenpeace that Homebush Bay, the main Olympic site, is contaminated with highly toxic dioxin, the legacy of a former Union Carbide factory manufacturing the 'Agent Orange' herbicide 2,4,5-T. Fishing has been banned since 1990 in the bay, which is estimated to have the highest level of dioxin contamination of any waterway in the world. It later emerged that the government had covered up an investigation on the dumped chemicals whilst it was preparing its Olympic bid. Greenpeace claims that even the proposed multimillion dollar clean-up of the bay, scheduled to start in November 1998 and finish in December 1999, will not be enough to eliminate the effects of the poison. The 'green Olympics' received a further blow in October 1997, with a new report showing that the bay had record levels of dioxin contamination with a toxic rating 1500 times higher than accepted levels for residential areas.

tion is to convert it into a permanent international garden and tourist attraction once the festival is over. Mt Penang is fifty minutes by road from Sydney, eighty minutes by rail and bus link. A high-speed ferry service is also planned.

Nursery Industry Association of Australia, PO Box 907, Epping, New South Wales 2121 Ⓣ 1800/252-468 (toll-free) Ⓕ 02/9876 6360
Ⓦ http://www1.tpgi.com.au/users/ncrowe/PE2000A.htm

TRAVEL BRIEF

Australia and New Zealand together are undoubtedly *the* destination for the year 2000, and many people visiting one will also take the opportunity to visit the other. Expect difficulties with both flights and accommodation all year.

GETTING THERE Australia has two main airlines, Qantas and the largely domestic Ansett Australia, although many other major carriers also have services from around the world, most flying direct to Sydney. Ansett, the official carrier for the Olympic Games, is arranging extra domestic services to ensure full availability, but there are unlikely to be additional longhaul services owing to the difficulties of getting route licences. Book as far ahead as possible and when in doubt, try other Australian gateways.

ACCOMMODATION There are likely to be severe accommodation shortages in Sydney during the Olympics, with around 50,000 beds currently available, an estimated 160,000 needed and a 10-percent bed tax to help pay for the Games. As well as the new building currently underway, ships will be anchored in the harbour as floating hotels, and locals are being encouraged to open their doors for rentals and B&B. Expect to pay premium prices for apartment and house rentals. SOCOG has two official private home rental programmes, Homehost (B&B accommodation for athletes and their families) and Homestay, which will offer vacant, furnished houses and apartments. The official agent for Homestay is: Ray White Real Estate, PO Box 5200, Sydney NSW 2001 Ⓣ 02/9262 3700 Ⓕ 9262 3737; within Australia: Ⓣ 1-800/646 766. Home exchanges are worth considering. Try home exchange bureaux in your home country or Web sites such as:
Ⓦ http://www.sydneycity.net/directory/accomguide.htm or
Ⓦ http://www.holi-swaps.com or
Ⓦ http://www.sydney.auscape.net/accom.html

Olympic tickets: Tickets for the Games will be on sale to the public in late 1998, and for the Paralympic Games in 1999. You can register in advance with the official ticket agencies, who will also be providing a variety of

packages to the Games. UK: Sportsworld ⓣ 01235/554 844. New Zealand:
Sportsworld International, ⓣ 09/307 0770. South Africa: Sportsworld Events
and Tours ⓣ 11/646 4862.

TOURIST OFFICES National: Level 4, 80 William St, Wooloomooloo,
Sydney, NSW 2011 ⓣ 02/9360 1111 ⓕ 9331 3385; New South Wales:
11–31 York St, Sydney, NSW 200 ⓣ 02/132 077 ⓕ 9224 4411.
UK: London ⓣ 0181/780 2229; Aussie Help-line ⓣ 0990/561 434.
US: New York ⓣ 212/687 6300; Los Angeles ⓣ 310/229 4870.
ⓦ http://www.aussie.net.au/ (tourism)
ⓦ http://www.sydney.olympic.org/ (Olympics).

COUNTRY CODE ⓣ 61

BELGIUM

Belgium has no official plans for the millennium beyond
what has been planned in the EC government-dominat-
ed city of Brussels.

Brussels

As one of the **European Cities of Culture 2000**, Brussels is
aiming to recast its stodgy image and to project a more
dynamic, multicultural side to itself.

The theme of **Brussels 2000** is 'The City' and during 1997
over 3000 people participated in an extensive consultation
exercise to find out how best to revitalise the city's cultural life.

Projects under discussion include the creation of a central
cultural centre in the former Vanderborght building on
Schildnaapstraat; restoring the Palace of the Fine Arts and the

Royal Flemish Theatre; creating multicultural meeting places in local communities; refurbishing public spaces and squares with more public art; creating a 'contemporary nomadic infrastructure' (a sort of travelling art space which would move between districts); and building two new halls, one for opera and the other for dance and theatre.

Bruxelles/Brussels 2000, Quai de Commerce 18 Handelskaai, Bruxelles 1000, Belgium ⓣ 02/219 0019 ⓕ 218 7453.

European Cities of Culture 2000

Brussels is one of nine European Cities of Culture in the year 2000, the others being Avignon, Bergen, Bologna, Kraków, Helsinki, Prague, Reykjavik and Santiago de Compostela. The original idea for European Cities of Culture was conceived in 1983 by the then Greek minister of culture, Melina Mercouri, and it was formally adopted by the European Council of Ministers in 1985. Since then twelve cities have enjoyed the increased status and large EU grants which the title attracts, although not always with positive results. Thessaloniki, for instance, had this honour in 1997 but the celebrations were dogged by allegations of corruption and mismanagement over the 80-billion drachma budget (£170,000/US$277,000), and an official inquiry was instigated to find out where the money has disappeared to. The nine European Cities of Culture are working together to co-ordinate their programmes and to organise 'a European cultural space for the year 2000'. One manifestation of this is the ARCEUnet project, a joint programme involving Bergen, Bologna, Kraków and Santiago de Compostela, which aims to link together by satellite all the main museums and cultural institutions in each city into a vast 'virtual museum', where visitors will be able to browse among art works, architecture, sculpture and other cultural treasures in any of the cities.

TRAVEL BRIEF

Most tourism in Belgium is centred on Brussels and the medieval cities of Bruges and Ghent. The pattern seems unlikely to change in 2000, with Brussels as one of Europe's many cultural capitals. There may also be some celebrations connected with the jewellery trade in Antwerp.

GETTING THERE Advance booking over the New Year 2000 holiday may be advisable. There are numerous flights into Brussels from all major and many minor European airports as well as longhaul destinations, including several large US cities. There are frequent, fast rail links between Brussels and Paris, Amsterdam, London and other European cities.

ACCOMMODATION The presence of the EU, NATO and other major organisations means that Brussels has more than its fair share of expensive business hotels. As ever, book well ahead for major public holidays in Brussels, Bruges and Ghent.

TOURIST OFFICES National: 61 Rue Marché-aux-Herbes (also known as Grasmarkt), B-1000 Brussels Ⓣ 02/504 0200 Ⓕ 513 6950 (French-speaking area); Ⓣ 02/504 0300 Ⓕ 513 8803 (Flemish-speaking area); Brussels: Hôtel de Ville, Grand-Place Ⓣ 02/513 8940.
UK: London Ⓣ 0891/887 799 (premium rate). US: New York Ⓣ 212/758 8130.
Ⓦ http://www.touristoffices.org.uk/Belgium/index.html

COUNTRY CODE Ⓣ 32

BRAZIL

B razil has no national plans but **Rio de Janeiro** is likely to be a hot ticket for New Year's Eve 1999 – it was recently voted amongst the top five destinations in the world where people would like to party on that date, according to a survey by a German tour operator. Any celebration as big as

Brazil's **Carnaval** is likely to be a popular option in 2000, and although Carnaval parades take place all over the country, the biggest draw is always Rio's spectacular parade.

Rio

New Year's Eve in Rio de Janeiro is marked with special celebrations, since the turning of the year is also the feast day of **Iemanjá**, the goddess of the sea. Cariocas, the majority of them dressed in white, descend in their thousands to Copacabana Beach to place candlelit offerings in the surf for Iemanjá. The ceremonies are followed by a major fireworks display over the bay at midnight; for 1999 there are proposals for a spectacular laser show as well.

From New Year's Eve onwards preparations begin for Carnaval, building up to a week of intense revelry with numerous Carnaval balls (*bailes carnavalescos*) and culminating in the parade of samba schools for which Rio is famous. In 2000, Carnaval takes place in the week leading up to March 5, when the parade takes place.

TRAVEL BRIEF

GETTING THERE Rio is served by most of the world's airlines as well as the Brazilian carriers Varig, Vasp and Transbrasil, with direct flights from more than seventy countries.

ACCOMMODATION Rio has more than 200 hotels but they are likely to be very heavily booked well in advance of New Year's Eve 1999 and Carnaval 2000. Other accommodation options include private house and apartment rentals.

TOURIST OFFICES Riotur, 9th floor, Rua da Assembléia 10, Rio de Janeiro 20011-001 ⓣ / ⓕ 021/531 1231. Brazil has no national overseas Tourist OfficeS; enquiries are handled by embassies and consulates.

COUNTRY CODE ⓣ 55

BRITAIN

B ritain is set for a millennium boom. Nowhere else is offering so huge a range of millennial attractions and facilities, from state-of-the-art science and cultural centres to millennium forests, cycle tracks, stadiums, public squares, bridges, and environmental schemes. Many of these are intended to benefit local communities, but numerous others, particularly in London, are major visitor attractions in their own right and are expected to draw in millions of overseas tourists in 1999 and 2000. The **British Tourist Authority** is already promoting Britain as 'the world's leading millennium destination' and **London**, with its mega-projects – the Millennium Dome, Bridge and Wheel – will clearly have much to justify the claim.

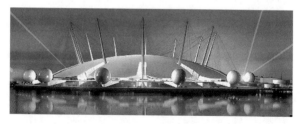

Who is responsible for this millennium boom? The finger points at an unlikely source – the former Conservative prime minister John Major. His policies may be all but forgotten but it was his decision to set up a **National Lottery** which led to the creation of the **Millennium Commission**, one of five 'good causes' supported by the lottery. The success of the lottery has given the Millennium Commission an estimated £2 billion (US$3.3b) to spend on projects to mark the year 2000 – a sum that dwarfs other national budgets.

The Commission has supported four main types of projects: **Landmark Capital Projects**, of which there are fourteen, intended as landmarks for the twenty-first century in England, Scotland, Wales and Northern Ireland; **Local or Regional Capital Projects**, of which there are hundreds, including 'umbrella schemes' covering projects all over the UK; the **Millennium Exhibition and Festival**; and the **Millennium Awards**, intended to fulfil 'more personal aspirations for the next century'. By December 1997 the Commission had awarded a total of £1.2 million (US$2m) to almost 200 projects on 2800 sites around Britain.

With such large sums at stake, the Millennium Commission has not been immune to criticism, particularly concerning the **Millennium Exhibition at Greenwich** (see pp.62–63). Additionally, all the grants made by the Millennium Commission are dependent on the bid organisers raising an equal amount in the private sector or other grant sources. Dozens of projects have been trying to tap the same sources of money and it's likely that many will never see the light of day, or they may open well beyond the year 2000. But the millennium will still see hundreds of British projects completed, including around 250 millennium Greens, the revival of 122 miles of canals and waterways, 1000 new woodland and forest areas, and 100 new town fountains.

One of the most extensive national projects is the creation of **Millennium Routes**, a network of over 2500 miles of cycle paths being co-ordinated by the Bristol-based **Sustrans** group. A combination of traffic-free paths on disused railways, towpaths and tracks and routes on minor or 'traffic-calmed' roads, the network is due to open on June 21, 2000. The Millennium Routes are part of a much larger **National Cycle Network**, planned to cover 6500 miles by the year

2005. The completion of the Millennium Routes will be celebrated with local and national rides, a time trail, and treasure hunts and projects for children.

Other significant environmental projects for 2000 include the **Groundwork Foundation**'s transformation of wasteland sites into woodlands, wetlands or recreational facilities; **Woods on Your Doorstep**, a Woodland Trust programme for new community woods, and **Yews for the Millennium**. The latter is a neat, appropriate project. Known as the tree of life to the Celts, yews can live for thousands of years; they were often the focal point of pagan rituals and later became synonymous with parish churchyards.

All 3000 sites throughout Britain which have benefited from Millennium Commission funds will be able to display the Commission's logo, 'The Big M'.

Throughout Britain the arrival of the millennium will be marked by a nationwide peal of bells in churches, chapels and towers, as well as a switching-on ceremony for specially installed floodlights on over 400 churches. The Church of England is also planning to distribute candles to every household in the land.

On the morning of Sunday, January 2, 2000 there will be a State Millennium Service in **St Paul's Cathedral**, and Sir Cliff Richard and other celebrities will be performing in a multimedia celebration in London as part of the 'Fanfare for a New Generation' campaign to reclaim the millennium for

Beacon Millennium

Beacons have been in use for centuries as a means of communication. In ancient Greece, beacons lit on the tops of a chain of eight mountains spread the news of the Fall of Troy across the country in a single night, and in Britain the Romans used them on Hadrian's Wall to warn of attacks by Picts and Scots. In the sixteenth century they were a vital part of the English coastal warning system against the Spanish Armada.

Beacons have also been used throughout history to celebrate joyful events. In Britain these have included Queen Victoria's Golden Jubilee in 1887, Queen Elizabeth II's Silver Jubilee in 1977 and most recently the Celebration of VE Day in 1994.

The organiser of that event, Bruno Peak, has now set his sights on an ambitious plan for Beacon Millennium, which he hopes will involve the lighting of more than a million beacons all over the world to mark the arrival of the year 2000. He envisages a chain of bonfire beacons, beacon braziers and gas-lit beacons (as well as 'virtual beacons' on the Internet) which will become part of 'a worldwide social event, a communal act unprecedented in human history'.

Beacon Millennium is working with a number of charities and educational trusts and it is also hoping to stage a national Peace Run, with participants carrying lighted torches (similar to the Olympic torch) to the four capital cities of the UK where the main beacons at midnight on December 31, 1999 will be lit.

Beacon Millennium, West Park, Rockbourne, Fordingbridge, Hampshire SP6 3JB ☎ 01725/518 810.

Christianity. The Archbishop of Canterbury is also planning a series of **Holy Raves** in May 1999 and has booked Wembley Arena, the Royal Albert Hall and three London cathedrals for the celebrations. The event, called 'The Time of Our Lives', will involve over 10,000 young people in a weekend of rock music, cabaret and comedy presented by Christian artists, as well as 'alternative' services in the three cathedrals.

Millennium Commission, Portland House, Stag Place, London SW1E 5EZ
Ⓣ 0171/880 2001 Ⓕ 880 2000 Ⓦ http://www.millennium.gov.uk
Explains the background and aims of the UK's Millennium Commission.
Includes their Millennium Map, with descriptions of grant-aided projects and
details on the Millennium Awards and Millennium Festival.

TS^{2}k: Trafalgar Square 2000

Trafalgar Square 2000 is a project to help London's young unemployed by providing career routes into the creative industries – media, entertainment and new technology – through several Creative Enterprise Centres being set up across the capital (the first opened in Brixton in November 1997). The public centrepiece of the project will be a major programme of multimedia events through the year 2000.

Trafalgar Square 2000, Toynbee Studios, 26 Commercial Street,
London E1 6LS Ⓣ 0171/247 4994.

LONDON

London has got millennium fever. Even taking big projects such as Sydney's Olympics 2000 and Hannover's Expo 2000 into acccount, no other city can equal its vast number of projects under construction or being planned. They may have little to do with the celebration of Christ's birth, but the city is about to acquire the **Millennium Dome, Millennium Wheel, Millennium Bridge, Millennium Villages**, and much more besides. Over £4 billion (US$6.5b) is being invested in the capital's leisure industries in the run-up to 2000, with around fifty new hotels under construction.

Part of the reason is, of course, that London includes the historic borough of **Greenwich**, the 'home of time', thanks to its status as the **Prime Meridian of the World** from where time all over the globe is measured. The sun might rise first in the South Pacific but the start of the new day, as the clock ticks past midnight on December 31, 1999 into the first millisecond of January 1, 2000, will most definitely be at Greenwich.

London's traditional focus for New Year's Eve revels, **Trafalgar Square**, will be eclipsed at the millennium by events in Greenwich when the dome opens on December 31, 1999.

Greenwich

Celebrations at **Greenwich** will take place in two separate locations. The first of these is on the **Greenwich Peninsula**, 300 acres of derelict wasteland (formerly one of Europe's largest gas works); the second is in the **historic centre of Greenwich** itself, about a mile distant.

Greenwich, Time and the Meridian

Greenwich, the 'official home of world time', has associations with time-keeping dating back to the seventeenth century, with Charles II's appointment of John Flamsteed as the first Astronomer Royal and the founding of the famous Royal Observatory. Flamsteed's task was to study the positions of the stars, the moon and the planets, with the aim of discovering an astronomical method of finding the longitude of a ship at sea. This was becoming an increasingly urgent requirement, as maritime nations such as Britain set out to explore and map the oceans.

By the mid-nineteenth century it was also becoming apparent that an international system of time-keeping was needed, partly due to the expansion of communications and transport systems such as the railways. Previously, almost every town and region in the world kept its own time. In 1852 Britain adopted 'London time', essentially, Greenwich Mean Time (GMT), although this was not adopted formally by Parliament until August 2, 1880. At noon on November 18, 1883 the United States followed suit, adopting GMT and transmitting the time signal by telegraph to all major cities. Prior to this, the US had over 300 local time zones. The Greenwich Meridian became a standard the following year.

A meridian is a north-south line used as a base point for astronomical observations, and thus for the calculation of longitude and time. There were so many different meridians in use around the world that the president of the United States called the International Meridian Conference in Washington, DC in October 1884 to decide where the prime meridian should be. Forty-one delegates from 25 nations attended.

During the conference the delegates chose Greenwich as the Prime Meridian of the World by a vote of 22-1. The International Date Line was then drawn up and 24 time zones created. The Prime Meridian is defined by the position of the 'Transit Circle' telescope in the Observatory's Meridian building; the cross-hairs in the eyepiece of the Transit Circle precisely define longitude 0° for the world.

Greenwich became the Prime Meridian for two reasons, the first of which was that the US had already adopted a system based on Greenwich Mean Time. The second was that by this period Greenwich's earlier expertise had ensured that 72 percent of the world's seafarers used charts based on the Greenwich meridian. Naming Greenwich as longitude 0° essentially solved the problem whilst inconveniencing the least number of people.

In the courtyard of the Old Royal Observatory at Greenwich a brass bar in the ground marks the Prime Meridian, 0° longitude. If there's one place in the world where you can be sure of knowing where you are, it should be here. And to the north of the Observatory, the New Millennium Experience is confidently planning a spire on Meridian Point in the Meridian Gardens to the west side of the Dome.

Unfortunately, the meridian has moved. Today, longitudes are defined by a differential Global Positioning Receiver, fed by a fleet of US military satellites, and this system places the meridian 336ft to the east of that brass strip at Greenwich. The WGS84 grid became the global standard for air navigation on January 1, 1988.

The New Millennium Experience is sticking with the Airy Meridian, although purists argue that this is a backward-looking approach which ignores advances in global mapping and the correct position as accepted by the international scientific community.

Ⓦ http://www.ast.cam.ac.uk/
The Royal Greenwich Observatory's pages contain a vast wealth of data on everything connected to astronomy and time.

Ⓦ http://www.greenwich2000co.uk/millennium/index.html
Describes plans for celebrations in historic Greenwich and sponsorship opportunities.

The compelling story of how the clockmaker John Harrison eventually solved the time-keeping problem is told in the bestselling book *Longitude* by Dava Sobel (Fourth Estate; Walker Pub. Co; 1995).

The Dome and the Millennium Exhibition

After seven years of planning, political wrangling and savagings by the media, Greenwich's **Millennium Dome** will finally open on December 31, 1999. Acting as a national lightning conductor for premillennial tensions, the Dome has attracted enormous criticism since architect Richard Rogers first unveiled his plan for what he descibed as "an odyssey into the future, a twenty-first century Stonehenge".

When Greenwich was first chosen as the exhibition site in 1996 fears were expressed that the peninsula, riddled with toxic chemicals from over a century of heavy industrial use, would never be cleaned up sufficiently. In 1997 **Greenpeace** successfully campaigned against the Dome's PVC roof, claiming that it would create a "toxic, plastic throwaway monster", and the government was forced to abandon it in favour of a glass-fibre and Teflon coating at an extra cost of £8 million (US$13m). The Dome also became a political football between the Tory and Labour parties as concern mounted over its escalating budget, and the organisers were forced to dramatically cut costs.

Despite an increasingly hostile press, construction of the Dome continued, with the first of the 105-tonne steel masts hoisted into place in October 1997. The building itself is due to be completed in late 1998, but the government is still seeking £120m (US$195m) in private sponsorship to offset the costs. Sponsors signed up so far include British Airways and British Telecom and, in an effort to give the project a more global appeal, there are plans to include displays sponsored by Microsoft and Japanese corporations such as Sony, Toshiba and Nissan.

The Dome will open with a huge gala night, rock concert, and laser and fireworks displays. The audience of 35,000 will consist of both invited VIPs and the general public. Amongst those attending will be the Queen, the Duke of Edinburgh, the Prince of Wales and prime minister Tony Blair.

Tickets are likely to sell out almost as soon they're available. Greenwich residents will be getting special previews, but for the general public it will be the first opportunity to find out what all the fuss has been about and to give their verdict on the long-awaited 'millennium experience'.

The opening will be broadcast live by the BBC, revealing for the first time the sheer scale and ambition of a project that dwarfs any other monument to the millennium built anywhere on the planet.

The Dome's translucent canopy, 1km in circumference, will glow in the Greenwich night sky, suspended by a web of twelve vast, yellow steel masts. An unmistakable statement of millennial confidence, Richard Roger's design will be a visual triumph, and gratifyingly telegenic to boot. The interior, with its enormous 50m-high canopy creating a vast canvas for special effects, will be breathtaking.

Inside, a central plaza will form the stage for a multimedia spectacular combining live performers and hi-tech wizardry. The show, on the theme of Time, will have a 'carnival atmosphere' and be visible by everyone in the Dome. The original plans called for an enclosed central arena, but abolishing this has opened up the show to take in the whole of the Dome. Performances will take place at frequent intervals, so you can watch it whilst browsing around the rest of the displays.

Around the central plaza there will be an outer ring divided into twelve segments, each representing a 'street' in time. Each zone will pose questions about the way we live, work, eat, play and interact with the environment and the rest of the world. The exhibition will use interactive exhibits, virtual reality displays (including a 'virtual forest') and 'dark rides' (of the kind used at France's Futuroscope) to engage audiences in what they hope is an 'entertaining, inspirational, educational and fun' experience, exploring the futuristic world of the next millennium. It will ask questions such as 'Will we still live in houses?' and 'Does God exist?'

Artists such as Damien Hirst and David Hockney have also been involved in creating backdrops for the interior, which will incorporate exhibits such as the **Valley of the Ladders**, symbolising career paths in the next century; the **Tower of Serious Play**, in which visitors will move on conveyor belts past interactive holograms; and **Our Town**, where 365 towns and villages will be invited to create a display for a day. There will be quiet rooms for contemplation and terminals for accessing a national oral history project, the **Millennium**

The Drumming Pulse

Despite the tight-lipped silence on the contents of the Dome which drove the press into a hostile frenzy during 1997, one fact did emerge: there will be a drum show, possibly as part of the multimedia spectacular in the central plaza. Paris is also hoping to have two thousand drummers as part of their egg-laying cere-mony beneath the Arc de Triomphe. In America, Global Drum-ming 2000 groups in Boston, New Mexico and elsewhere are planning a network of drum circles with Japanese Teiko drum-mers, Indian tabla players, and percussionists from Havana to Kinshasa all reaching a crescendo at midnight. Drummers will be ushering in the dawn on Pacific islands. Drumming, it seems, will be the musical pulse of the millennium.

Challenge, which will digitally record people's experiences of life at the end of the twentieth century.

The Dome will also feature what has been billed as the 'twenty-first century sport' – **surfball**, details of which were not available as we went to press, but which is said to meld 'surfing and ball skills'. There are also plans for a 30ft steel sphere, suspended above the ground by giant magnets, as well as displays on British history and exhibits from the British Museum. Amidst the giant video screens and clouds of dry ice there will also be a vast, three-dimensional human figure, which visitors will be able to step into.

Astronomers are also hoping to build a 2m robot telescope, which will be located in Hawaii and linked up to giant video screens in the Dome allowing visitors to share in the discov-ery of new comets, exploding stars and planetary systems as they take place. A computer terminal linked to star catalogues is also planned, enabling visitors to search for asteroids and name them.

In response to criticism from the church that the Dome contents are 'too secular', organisers stressed in early 1998 that the impact of Christianity on western civilisation would be a key theme. There are plans to display puppets and sets from *The Jesus Story*, an animated feature film being made to emphasise the Christian significance of the year 2000, which will be released in 1999.

Full details on the Dome's contents were due to have been announced in February 1998.

Ⓦ http://www.mx2000.co.uk/thedome.htm
Home pages of Greenwich's Millennium Dome, with details on who is building it, what may go inside it, and how UK residents can join in by taking part in the Millennium Challenge.

Meridian Point and Millennium Plaza

To the west of the dome is the **Meridian Point**, which will provide a focus for the surrounding **Meridian Gardens**, the main gateway to the exhibition for visitors arriving by boat. A performance space and visitor facilities will be created here. Curving around the outside of the Dome, the **Millennium River Walk** will offer views down towards the Thames Barrier.

The other main entrance to the Dome is in the **Millennium Plaza**, which is to have a new combined bus/underground station by 1998. Beyond the Millennium Plaza the **Millennium Park** and **Millennium Lakes** will lead through to the Millennium Village.

Millennium Village

The **Millennium Village** is a separate development to the exhibition intended to provide an environmentally and technically advanced urban village on the peninsula. The 32-acre site will initially have around 1000 homes, constructed using state-of-the-art energy efficiency building techniques. Community facilities such as schools, shops, health centres, pubs and restaurants are also being built. Facilities for cars will be kept to a minimum, but there are plans for a river bus service as well as an automatic transit system. Work is expected to start in summer 1998 on the £60 million (US$98m) scheme, which will ultimately allow for 5000 homes on a 296-acre site.

Greenwich Declaration

According to press reports, the government is planning to invite all 185 United Nations heads of state to London for the millennium to sign a Greenwich Declaration. Government representatives have been outlining what they see as a Magna Carta for the twenty-first century, which would embrace 'achievable aims' such as fresh water supply worldwide, greater literacy, improved living standards and a reduction in global pollution by the year 2020. The declaration will be signed on the historic site of the Meridian Line on December 31, 1999.

Historic Greenwich

Greenwich town (where the tea-clipper Cutty Sark is moored) and the adjacent **Greenwich Park** together form the historic centre of Greenwich. Within the park are several famous listed buildings, highlighting the importance of the town's astronomical and maritime heritage. These include the **Old Royal Observatory**, the **National Maritime Museum** and the **Queen's House**.

Meridian 2000

The National Maritime Museum of Greenwich is promoting **Greenwich Meridian 2000**, which will feature a New Year's Eve party extending across the whole of Greenwich Park for around 50,000 people. The BBC will be using it as their base for the worldwide telecasts and there will be giant screens here, as there will be at the Dome itself and in Trafalgar Square, relaying the parties and dawn ceremonies as they occur around the world.

As part of Greenwich Meridian 2000 there will be a prestigious new **Story of Time** exhibition at the National Maritime Museum, which will have eleven new galleries when redevelopment is complete in 1999.

GREENWICH MERIDIAN 2000"

The exhibition is designed to bring together 'significant historical artifacts' from museums around the world.

Greenwich Meridian 2000, 7G The Leathermarket, Weston Street, London
SE1 3ER Ⓣ 0171/357 7762 Ⓕ 357 7762
Ⓦ http://www.greenwich2000.com/countdown/meridian2000.htm

GREENWICH TRAVEL BRIEF

GETTING THERE The Millennium Experience will have its own Jubilee line tube station (journey time from central London around twelve minutes). Designed by Sir Norman Foster, the tube station is the largest ever constructed in Europe and can handle up to 22,000 passengers an hour. Nearly 40 percent of visitors are expected to arrive by tube. Car facilities will be severely limited.

The organisers are hoping that at least 1.6 million people will arrive by river boat: Greenwich town is currently served by services from piers at Westminster (fifty minutes), Charing Cross (forty-five minutes) and the Tower of London (thirty minutes). As well as a pier at the site itself, two new piers are being proposed for Waterloo on the south bank and Blackfriars on the north bank, with services running every ten–fifteen minutes during peak periods.

There will also be park-and-sail sites at Barking Reach and Woolwich Arsenal, and park-and-ride sites at Thamesmead, Falconwood and Canning Town. A Millennium Transit will operate from Charlton station on the North Kent Line. There are also proposals for a high-level, aerial cable car which would provide access from the north bank of the Thames. The site will be accessible from Greenwich town centre by bus, foot, bike and taxi.

   Greenwich town centre can be reached by train from Charing Cross, Waterloo East, or London Bridge (journey time around seventeen minutes). The Docklands Light Railway extension underneath the Thames to a new station at Cutty Sark (and on to Lewisham) is due to open in early 2000. Bus numbers 188 and 53 run from central London.

TOURIST OFFICES Greenwich Tourist Information Centre, 46 Greenwich Church Street, London SE10 9BL Ⓣ 0181/858 6376 Ⓕ 853 4607; Visitor Centre: The Millennium Experience Visitor Centre, Royal Naval College, Greenwich, London SE10 Ⓣ 0181/305 3546. Open 11am–7pm Mon-Fri, 10am–6pm weekends.

Ⓦ http://www.greenwich2000.com/ or Ⓦ http://www.greenwich2000.co.uk (UK edition)

Award-winning site that contains over 1000 pages on everything related to Greenwich, the meridian, time and the millennium. There is also a useful and practical travel and tourism section.

COUNTRY CODE Ⓣ 44

Millennium-on-Thames

One of London's greatest millennium projects is the revival of the **River Thames**. An array of prestigious millennium landmarks, from the **Millennium Dome** in Greenwich to the **Millennium Wheel** at Lambeth, is appearing on the south side of the river; the old Battersea Power Station is to be converted into a new entertainment complex and the South Bank Centre is to be entirely revamped, forming part of a **'Millennial Mile'** along the embankment. Plans are also underway to either build or restore several bridges.

   In addition, the government is pushing forward proposals to make the most of the city's artery by creating a new **river bus system**. The scheme calls for ten new piers and a fleet of privately run high-speed ferries, with through-ticketing to link in to public transport. London already has fourteen piers; two more are in the pipeline – one at the New Millennium

Experience and one at the Globe Theatre. A further eight would be added at strategic locations, serving the Millennium Wheel, the Tate Gallery, Battersea and the Oxo Tower. Cruise liners will also be able to dock at a new £80 million (US$130m) terminal complex in Greenwich.

Millennium Ice Fair

According to a report in *The Observer* newspaper in London, a team of architects and engineers have drawn up plans to celebrate the dawn of the new century by holding an Ice Fair on a frozen River Thames. A mixture of glycol and water would be used to freeze a half-kilometre long stretch of the river, and the resulting ice blocks would be anchored in place between Charing Cross and the South Bank. "You would never forget the millennium if that was the year you could walk across the Thames", said architect Don Gray.

In medieval times Frost Fairs were frequently held on the Thames, and the scheme has already won the approval of the Guildhall library's specialist on Frost Fairs, Jeremy Smith. But a Port of London spokesman failed to see the fun side of it: "It would cause serious navigation problems", he commented.

The Millennium Wheel

Rivalling the Millennium Dome downstream at Greenwich, the **Millennium Wheel** will be operating from late summer 1999 on a site parallel to Jubilee Gardens on the south bank directly opposite the Houses of Parliament.

Supported above the waters of the Thames by a cantilevered structure, the 151m-high Millennium Wheel, weighing 2240 tonnes, will be the largest Ferris wheel ever built. It is intended not only as a symbol of the passing of time (with its sixty capsules reflecting seconds and minutes), but is also intended to be a showcase for 'green technology', drawing on renewable sources to power half of the 150kW daily requirement of its turbines. It will also be virtually noiseless. Views of the capital and the countryside will extend as far as Royal Tunbridge Wells and Guildford in the south, Windsor in the west, Luton and Stansted in the north, and Gravesend and Rochester in the east.

Architects David Marks and Julia Barfield have designed the wheel in collaboration with engineers **Ove Arup Partners**, and it is being underwritten by British Airways, who have provided £600,000 (US$980,000) towards the estimated £10 million (US$16.3m) building cost. Two million visitors a year are expected to be carried in sixty enclosed cabins, each with six-

teen seats, on a ride 'no rougher than a children's swing' lasting about twenty minutes. Personal headsets will provide the commentary in a choice of languages as the wheel revolves at the sedate speed of just one foot per second. At the end of five years, the structure will be dismantled and moved to a new permanent home.

Such an ambitious and conspicuous structure on London's skyline has invited its fair share of criticism. Members of the public have suggested that it will spoil the view from many of London's parks; some MPs have expressed concern that passengers may be able to see into the Houses of Parliament, while others are worried that the wheel may become a permanent fixture.

But most commentators seemed to like the concept of the wheel, including the *Sunday Times* (London), which described it as "one of those maverick projects that bears the hallmark of a 'good idea'. It is slightly silly, but then most great monuments have an element of the absurd: Nelson's Column, the Eiffel Tower, the Statue of Liberty."

The Wheel was granted planning permission in 1996; construction began in spring 1998.

Tickets are expected to be around £5 (US$8) with children half-price and special rates for families, groups and pensioners. There will be full access for the disabled. Ticket sales, a visitors' centre and gift shop will be in the former County Hall building next to the London Aquarium.
Further information ℗ 0171/738 8080.

The Tate at Bankside

One of the fourteen **Landmark Projects** funded in part by the Millennium Commission will be the new **Tate Gallery of Modern Art** at Bankside, whose designers aim to 'celebrate the move from one millennium to the next by creating for the UK one of the world's three great museums of modern art'.

The first new national cultural institution to be built in London since the Royal National Theatre in the 1970s, the new gallery is to be housed inside a redundant power station in Southwark, opposite St Paul's Cathedral. The vast space within the shell of the old building, 35m high from basement to roof, will be converted into 20,000 square metres of naturally lit galleries. The scheme will also involve a multimedia information centre, shops, cafés, a rooftop restaurant and a 150m-long sheltered street in the old Turbine Hall.

The new gallery will house the Tate's collection of international twentieth-century art, including modern British art, as well as providing space for major touring exhibitions. The Tate's current premises at Millbank will become the **Tate Gallery of British Art**, showing British art from the sixteenth century to the present day. Refurbishment started in 1997, and the opening is planned for spring 2000.

House our Youth 2000

No one is sure how many young people are homeless in Britain (figures vary between 30,000 and 250,000), but the charity NCH Action for Children say that the problem is getting worse. In February 1997 they launched House our Youth 2000, the biggest campaign in the charity's 127-year history, with the aim of 'consigning the problem of youth homelessness to the twentieth century'. Their goal is to abolish youth homelessness by 2002, working together with the homeless, charities, clergy, local authorities and the government.

House our Youth 2000, NCH Action for Children, 85 Highbury Park, London N5 1UD ⓣ 0171/226 2033 ⓕ 226 2537. A campaign pack is available if you wish to help.

The Millennium Bridge

By the year 2000 the eye-catching **Millennium Bridge** will span the Thames from below St Paul's Cathedral on the north bank to the Bankside power station (the site of the new Tate Gallery of Modern Art) and the Globe Theatre on the south side. London's first new Thames crossing since Tower Bridge opened in 1894, it will also be the capital's first and only dedicated pedestrian bridge. The competition to design it, which attracted a record 226 entries from around the world, was won by sculptor Sir Anthony Caro in collaboration with the architect Sir Norman Foster.

The 4m-wide structure with a central span of 240m comprises an arc of stainless steel housing a deck of wooden

planks. Its minimalist horizontal lines will not be disrupted by lampposts or other paraphernalia, but will open up new views of London and St Paul's, with a viewing platform on the South Bank looking back towards the cathedral. The £10 million (US$16.3m) project will be completed by May 2000, at the same time as the new Tate Gallery of Modern Art.

Back to the Future

As debate raged about what to actually put inside the Dome, commentators turned to their history books for inspiration, focusing on the Great Exhibition of 1851, in effect the first ever 'World Fair'.

The Great Exhibition, the brainchild of Queen Victoria's idealistic consort, Prince Albert, was a hugely ambitious and exciting project, but the whole event was almost scrapped because no building could be found in which to stage it.

A solution was provided just in time by Joseph Paxton, gardener to the Duke of Devonshire, who at one time had designed a glass hothouse for his employer's water-lilies. Paxton's proposal was for something similar on a gigantic scale. It resulted in the exhibition hall at Hyde Park, whose iron structure, clad with 900,000 square feet of glass, came to be known as the Crystal Palace.

The Great Exhibition was a huge success, attracting six million visitors over five months. It featured over 100,000 exhibits ranging from the fine arts to new inventions, a celebration of Britain's scientific and technological prowess of the time. It also made a profit of £186,000 (US$303,000), which Prince Albert used to create today's South Kensington museums. The Crystal Palace itself was eventually moved to Sydenham, where it served as an exhibition centre until it was destroyed by fire in 1936.

The millennium has also been compared to the Festival of Britain of 1951, an event intended as a celebration of British design, architecture, art and the sciences, echoing the memory of the 1851 exhibition. It featured the first ever 3-D film, a gravity-defying Rotor, mechanical fountains, a Dome of Discovery and the extraordinary Skylon – a sculptured cigar-shaped tower pointing towards the heavens. Its lasting legacy was the Royal Festival Hall, which became the nucleus of today's South Bank Centre, Europe's largest arts centre.

The South Bank

The **South Bank Centre** may also be revamped as part of the ambitious 'millennial mile' scheme which is aiming to create an enclosed pedestrian space along the river embankment. If the project goes ahead, work should be completed by spring 2001. The oldest Gothic building in London, **Southwark Cathedral**, will have a new visitor centre and extended parks under the scheme.

Two new footbridges are also being built alongside the current **Hungerford Bridge**, linking Charing Cross with Waterloo on the south side of the river. The two new pier-like walkways are intended to make the most of Brunel's original brick piers. Pontoons for river boats and a floating restaurant are also part of the new plans.

Elsewhere in London

The **British Museum's** millennium project is the transformation of the 250-year-old building's central courtyard, the **Great Court**, into a covered square, providing a new cultural complex intended to rival the Louvre's glass pyramid.

Designed by Sir Norman Foster, the £72 million (US$117m) scheme includes the creation of a series of elliptical mezzanine floors around the Reading Room, with a 'spectacular walkway' spiralling around the outside, linking the Great Court with the upper floors of the museum. On a lower level, a new **Centre of Education** will offer a continuous programme of lectures, seminars and films and a new suite of galleries for the museum's African collections. At the centre of the Great Court, the **Round Reading Room** is to house an information centre on the museum's collections, open to the general public for the first time in its history. The entire courtyard will be enclosed by a translucent roof. Building work begins in 1998, for completion by the end of 2000.

In the city's East End architect Piers Gough is planning the revitalisation of **Mile End Park** with a novel Green Bridge which will unite the two halves of the park (currently separated by a busy road) by creating a massive steel-and-earth archway over the road, planted with trees on top. The scheme will also feature three wind generators, an art pavilion and an amphitheatre.

An (un)Dress Rehearsal for 2000

In the 1960s Timothy Leary had a vision that by the year 2000 cars would have vanished from Piccadilly to be replaced by grazing sheep and people strolling around naked. Impatience with the lack of progress towards this Arcadian vision led the group in this photograph to organise their own rehearsal in 1976, in the hope of popularising the concept. "The goats and cockerel were borrowed from the urban farm in Camden. It was early morning, and a few cars hooted. The police arrived just as the group was wrapped back in rugs", recalls one participant. No national paper would use the photo because of the naked men, but it did appear in the London magazine *Time Out*. Another nude Rehearsal for the Year 2000 will be held in the summer of 1999, they say.

London Zoo's millennium project is a £4.5 million (US$7.3m) Education Centre, a stunning glass pavilion, built from ecologically sound materials. Focusing on the conservation of biological diversity around the world, the centre will house a major collection of invertebrates, from jellyfish to crickets, crabs, starfish, spiders, snails and corals, alongside interactive displays and video walls.

In **Battersea** there are plans for a Millennium Village to be built on the site of a former parking lot near the river. The proposal, which is being developed by the Holy Trinity Brompton church, is to create a Christian landmark that will incorporate a celebration centre, a community village and a training and resource centre.

AROUND ENGLAND

As well as the numerous smaller projects taking shape in England, ten of the major Landmark Projects are being built at a total cost of over £600 million (US$980m).

Birmingham: Millennium Point

Located in Digbeth, Birmingham, **Millennium Point** aims to bring together learning, entertainment and real applications of science, technology and engineering to create a 'beacon for a new millennium, dedicated to stimulating a technologically capable and aware society'. Construction on the £110 million (US$180m) project is expected to start in 1998, with completion in June 2001.

The gateway to Millennium Point is the **Hub**, a series of linked public concourses with restaurants, cafés, exhibition and meeting areas and a 400-seater IMAX cinema. The primary attraction is the **Discovery Centre**, designed to integrate new technologies, historic and modern artifacts, interactive exhibits and multimedia displays in a three-dimensional network resembling a giant game of snakes and ladders where you can move vertically as well as horizontally through the exhibits. Themes will include Birmingham's industrial history, the development of science and technology in a global context, and a **Futures Gallery** featuring an interactive cinema which allows you to compare your vision of the future with the predictions of past luminaries such as H.G. Wells.

A **Showcase of British Manufacturing** will link the Discovery Centre with the **Technology Innovation Centre**, where laboratories and workshops will show research and development in action. There will also be a **University of the First Age**, which will include a young people's parliament, a library of educational futures, and facilities for young people to run their own local TV and radio channels.

Birmingham: Millennium Point, Council House, Victoria Square, Birmingham B1 1BB ⓣ 0121/235 4271 ⓕ 235 4317
ⓦ http://www.birmingham.gov.uk/millennium/

Bristol: Bristol 2000

The world's first electronic zoo, a virtual theatre and a museum of wildlife photography are some of the main features of the £82 million (US$133m) **Bristol 2000** project currently taking shape on ten acres of derelict land in the city's Harbourside area.

Wildscreen World will house the electronic zoo, combining live animal exhibits with interactive screens. It will also include the headquarters of **ARKive** (the world's first electronic archive of endangered species); a large format-cinema; a botanical house with free-flying tropical birds and insects; the museum of wildlife photography; and 'magic windows' which will be connected to remote cameras in wildlife reserves allowing real-time observation of larger animals in the wild.

Alongside Wildscreen World, **Science World** builds on the success of Bristol's Exploratory (Britain's first hands-on science centre set up in the 1980s). There will also be a series of 'plores' (scientific experiments presented as interactive exhibits) and a virtual theatre which will be used as a planetarium, 3D simulator and a science newsroom.

Wildscreen World and Science World are scheduled to open in spring 2000. The development will also include public squares, fountains, a new bridge and the **Harbourside Centre** – a purpose-built £93 million (US$152m) centre for the performing arts due to open in 2002.

Bristol: Bristol 2000, PO Box 2001, Bristol BS99 5TJ ℡ 0117/909 2000
🅕 909 9920 🆆 http://www.exploratory.org.uk/bris2000/

Doncaster: The Earth Centre

The **Earth Centre** aims to be the world's largest environmental visitor attraction, engaging millions of people in the vision of sustainable development. Most of the attractions are focused on a core twenty-acre site that will combine exhibitions, shows, interactive features, outdoor play and adventure areas, gardens and a showcase for futuristic technologies.

At the entrance to the Centre will be a vast solar canopy, the largest horizontal array of solar cells in Europe, providing up to 35 percent of the Earth centre's energy requirements. The **Planet Earth Galleries** will feature seven different

experiences based on 'visionary planet themes', a large wilderness play area and a 'spectacular light gallery'. **Future Works** is a cluster of pod-like buildings linked by the theme of making the future work for humankind and nature, featuring the **Millennium Cities Show, Eco-Station** and **Twenty First Century Living**.

Surrounding the main displays, the **Realm of the Senses** will incoporate a wetlands water ride, over 24 different gardens and a riverside wharf with cafés. There will also be a 400-seater **Earth Arena** and a **Water Works** building which will manage the water on site using hydroponic plant culture. The first part of the scheme is due to open in Easter 1999.

Doncaster: Earth Centre, Kilner's Bridge, Doncaster Road, Denaby Main, South Yorkshire DN12 4DY ⓣ 01709/512000 ⓕ 512010
ⓦ http://www.shef.ac.uk/ec/

Leicester: National Space Science Centre

Leicester is building the **National Space Science Centre**, which will include the first NASA-backed **Challenger Learning Centre** outside of the US offering simulated space

flights; an exhibition on the achievements and future potential of space travel; a planetarium in the shape of the Millennium Dome; a 35m tower containing space rockets and a research centre linked to the University of Leicester. The centre is due to open in early 2001.

Leicester: National Space Science Centre, University of Leicester, University Road, Leicester LE1 7RH Ⓣ 0116/252 2436 Ⓕ 252 5000
Ⓦ http://www.star.le.ac.uk/nssc/index.html

Newcastle: International Centre for Life

At the forefront of the industrial revolution in earlier centuries, Newcastle now hopes to reverse its current decline by placing itself at the leading edge of the twenty-first century with the **International Centre for Life**, a multipurpose complex that combines a research institute, commercial biotechnology centre and visitor centre dedicated to the genetics revolution.

The heart of the £54 million (US$88m) centre is the **Helix** discovery centre, which aims to explain genetics via a futuristic **Gene Dome** in which visitors will be 'shrunk' so they can journey through the human body. The centre will also include a **Timeline** spanning four billion years of genetic evolution and a **Health Quest** area which will encourage healthy lifestyle choices.

Alongside Helix there will be a research-based **Genetics Institute** and a **Biotechnology Centre** for commercial businesses. The International Centre for Life is backed by Newcastle University and the Tyne & Wear Development Corporation and has attracted £51 million (US$83m) in grants from the Millennium Commission, the European Regional Development Fund and other sources.

The centre has not avoided controversy, however, and fears have been expressed that it will simply gloss over moral and ethical issues such as the threat to disabled people from pre-natal screening of faulty genes. "The Centre for Life is about

F*ck the Millennium

In the autumn of 1997 travellers on London's Underground were confronted with black-and-white flyposted stickers which read simply 'F*ck the Millennium' and, soon afterwards, a full-page advert appeared in *The Guardian* newspaper to the same effect, inviting readers to phone in and decide Yes/No. "If you want to fuck the millennium, press one", intoned a polite voice, "if not, press two." An astonishing 18,500 people responded, around 90 percent of whom quite happily pressed button one to "fuck the millennium."

Who are the mysterious K2 Plant Hire who placed the ad? Step forward anarchic pranksters Jimmy Cauty and Bill Drummond, known in a previous incarnation as the band KLF, which later transmuted into an art project, the K Foundation, famous for burning £1 million (US$1.63m) cash from music earnings in 1995. The pair's comeback in 1997 was a live musical/theatrical presentation (universally panned by the critics) which became a single, 'Fuck the Millennium,' featuring a brass band and a bunch of unemployed Liverpool dockers chanting the title phrase.

And the phone-in? The vote, say K2 Plant Hire, has given them a mandate to take further action. A short time ago they revealed their plans on the Internet for the real millennium project – the Great Northern Pyramid of the People. Designed to stand 150ft high on a 300ft square base, the pyramid will be built from 'eighty-seven million, two hundred and fifty thousand bricks (roughly)'. This represents around one brick for every person born in the UK during the 20th century. K2 Plant Hire will arrange to collect the bricks, provided that people can help them out by finding 'as many abandoned bricks as they may have lying around in their gardens, behind their dustbins, being used as a door-stopper in the bog, or any of those other places where lost bricks may be found'.

The 'People's Pyramid' will be open 365 days a year, 24 hours a day, free of charge. "You'll be able to do what you want with it. Climb it, paint it, polish it, eat your sandwiches on it, or chip it away", they say. "It will stand for as long as any of it is left. It will promote nothing, be sponsored by nobody, and be owned by everybody."

The site has yet to be announced (and even then it may not pass the hurdle of planning permission), but it will not be in the Southeast of England. Building will commence, they say, at the beginning of the 21st century when they have an accurate figure of the 20th-century births to work on. Even if it never sees the light of day, the concept of the People's Pyramid is a brilliantly anarchic send-up of the values behind the multimillion-pound Millennium Dome.

Ⓦ http://www.k2planthire.ltd.uk/

genetic hype rather than genuine education and debate", says Dr Tom Shakespeare of the University of Leeds. "It plays the same propaganda role for biotechnology as the Sellafield Visitor Centre does for nuclear power."

The centre is hoping for around 300,000 annual visitors and is expected to open in March 2000.

Newcastle: International Centre for Life, Tyne & Wear Development Corporation, Scotswood House, Newcastle Business Park, Newcastle-upon-Tyne NE4 7YL ⓣ 0191/226 1234 ⓕ 226 1388 ⓔ iclgeneral@life-secret-2000.co.uk

Norwich: Technopolis

Opposite the cathedral in it's central square, Norwich is planning **New Technopolis**, a multipurpose centre that will include a **Millennium Library, Business and Learning Centre, Visitor Centre**, auditoriums, cafés, restaurants and other facilities.

Norwich Technopolis, Project Office, Castle Mall Management Suite, Norwich NR1 3DD ⓣ 01603/610524 ⓕ 610150 ⓔ normillbid@msn.com

Portsmouth: Harbour Renaissance

One of the largest projects in the southeast is the **Renaissance of Portsmouth Harbour**, an £86-million (US$140m) scheme which is due for completion in the summer of 2000. The main features of the project include a new marina, a 150m-high **Millennium Tower** with an observation gallery overlooking the harbour entrance, extensive promenades around the harbour, a new **Navy in Action** centre and **International Maritime Research Centre** in the Historic Dockyard, a new **National Museum of Armaments** in Gosport, and pontoons for a water bus service connecting Gosport and Portsmouth.

Portsmouth Harbour Renaissance, Civic Offices, Guildhall Square, Portsmouth PO1 2BG ⓣ 01705/834576 ⓕ 834938.

The Chalk Chip

The ancient symbolic figures cut centuries ago into the chalk hills of Britain may be joined by a twenty-first century equivalent – a giant Chalk Chip. The chip, 33m wide and 15m high, will be carved into a hillside and filled with chalk in the traditional fashion. The designer, Tom Newton, is touring the country during 1998 with a full-scale template of the fourteen-prong chip in an attempt to assess its impact on potential sites before building commences during the first half of 1999.

He is hoping to place the chip in a high-profile position where it will be visible from road, rail and air routes (from 35,000ft the chip's apparent size will be the same as an actual fourteen-prong microchip in a computer). The chip would be dug by hand rather than machine, and Newton plans to have an annual celebration and clean-up involving the local community at the site where it is placed. "But", says Newton, "it is emphatically not a glorification of the chip." The message is to 'pause and consider' the implications of microchip technology in the next millennium. "The only way forward now is by lateral and dynamic interaction with the microchip. It is a symbol of the millennium for the millennium" claims the designer.

Salford Quays: Lowry Centre

The **Lowry Centre** claims to be the first integrated cultural centre in the UK for the visual and performing arts, and will incorporate a display centre for the world's largest collection of works by the artist L.W. Lowry, the Lowry Study Centre, an exhibition gallery, two theatres and children's 'hands-on' art gallery. The centre is due to open in summer 2000.

Lowry Centre Project Office, Salford Civic Centre, Chorley Road, Swinton, Salford M27 5BW Ⓣ 0161/793 2486 Ⓕ 793 2813.

St Austell: The Eden Project

The **Eden Project** is an ambitious scheme to transform a clay pit near St Austell, Cornwall, into one of the biggest greenhouses in the world containing two 'biomes' – miniature ecosystems representing Mediterranean and tropical rainforest environments.

The £106 million (US$173m) project is the brainchild of Tim Smit, who has previously transformed a 100-acre Victorian estate in Cornwall, the **Lost Gardens of Heligan**, into one of the most popular private gardens in Britain, attracting 300,000 visitors a year.

The design of the massive greenhouse is a collaboration between Smit, his partner Jonathan Ball and the architect Nicholas Grimshaw, who was responsible for the striking S-shaped glass roof on the Eurostar terminal at Waterloo in London. The design has been adapted to the more complex contours of the clay pit, snaking over the 34-acre site with four greenhouses spanning up to 120m each, rising to 65m at the highest points to accommodate rainforest trees. The structure is to be covered with lightweight inflatable 'envelopes', which will be kept inflated by tiny solar-powered pumps. "It's the horticultural answer to the Taj Mahal or the Sydney Opera House", said Smit.

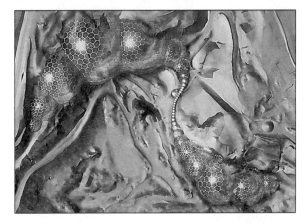

The project, which has received £37 million (US$60m) from the Millennium Commission and £10m (US$16.3m) from the European Regional Development Fund, will also include the Eden Botanical Institute, established to develop sustainable farming in rural communities. A visitor centre is expected to open in April 1999, followed by the 'biomes' in Easter 2000.

The environmental aims of the Eden Project seem to chime admirably with the millennium *Zeitgeist*, but the scheme has come under criticism from the local **Green Party** who claim that if the centre reaches its expected target of a million visitors a year, it will cause traffic problems in the surrounding area, since nearly all visitors will be arriving by car or coach.

Eden Project, Watering Lane Nursery, Pentewan, Cornwall PL26 6BE
Ⓣ 01726/222900 Ⓕ 222901.

Wakehurst Place: Millennium Seed Bank

For over twenty years the Royal Botanic Gardens at Kew has been collecting and storing plant seeds as a safeguard against the environmental destruction which is already threatening large swathes of the planet's genetic diversity. Botanists predict that as much as a quarter of the 250,000 species of flowering plants could become extinct over the next fifty years.

Although it boasts the most comprehensive collection in the world, Kew still only holds 2 percent of the earth's flora, and in order to improve on this, the **Millennium Seed Bank** is being built at Wakehurst Place in Sussex. The £75 million (US$122m) scheme aims to harvest all the flowering plants native to the UK by 1999 as well as 25,000 species of plants worldwide (10 percent of the world's flora) by 2010. Seeds will be collected from the wild, dried, and stored at sub-zero temperatures until needed. Alongside storage and scientific research facilities, the Seed Bank will also feature a public education centre, due to open in 2000.

For as little as £15 (US$24) you can help sponsor the collection of a particular species, and larger donors will have their names recorded in the Millennium Seed Book. The Millennium Seed Bank Appeal, PO Box 4370, London DW15 2PF ⓣ 0973/102000.

Elsewhere

Other millennium projects around England include:

BRADFORD: A new **National Faith Centre** will be built as part of the **Bradford Cathedral 2000 Project**.

CARLISLE: A **Millennium Gallery** will form part of the **Gateway City Project** to revitalise Carlisle's Roman and medieval heritage.

CHESTER: There are plans to build a **National Pondlife Centre** at Chester Zoo.

COVENTRY: Parts of the city centre will be rebuilt under a programme called **The Phoenix Initiative**, with public squares and spaces, including a **Millennium Boulevard** and a **Millennium Place**.

York Millennium Mystery Plays

Britain's oldest cycle of mystery plays is to be the focus of a high-profile production in the year 2000. The York Mystery Plays were created by the trade guilds in the eleventh century and were originally performed on wagons which trundled the players around the city centre. Revived in 1951, the plays traditionally feature local actors and take place in the central nave of York Minster. The Millennium Mystery Plays start on June 22, 2000 (Corpus Christi) and will run for four weeks, with around 25 performances. The York Early Music Festival takes place at the same time, and combined packages (including tickets, accommodation and rail travel) will be available. Tickets go on sale in autumn 1999.

Festival Office, PO Box 226, York YO3 6ZU Ⓣ 01904/658338 Ⓕ 612631 Ⓔ yemf@netcomuk.co.uk.

CUMBRIA: The **Renaissance of Whitehaven** project is to include an event centre, the **Hub**; a history centre, the **Quest**; and the **Crow's Nest**, 'a striking structure which will transmit a panoramic 3D view from the top of a 40m mast to the circular building at its base'.

DERBYSHIRE: The 200-square-mile **National Forest**, established in 1995, is to build a **Millennium Discovery Centre**, combining 'tactile experiences' with interactive technology depicting the changing world of forests, and a **National Forest Visitor Centre**, showing a 'living microcosm' of woodlands development as well as a **Millennium Events Arena** for celebrations in the year 2000.

DURHAM: There are plans for a **Millennium Hall** and also a **Millennium Square**.

HUDDERSFIELD: Plans are being considered for the restoration of the **Huddersfield Narrow Canal**.

Dressing up for the big Party

What will you be wearing to the big party on New Year's Eve 1999? The signs are that thousands will be flocking to their nearest costume hire shop, as invitations to fancy dress and themed parties begin to thud through the letterbox. But don't leave things until the last minute. Costume hire shops are predicting a millennial boom, with business expected to be 30–40 percent up on normal seasonal takings. Quick-buck merchants, operating from temporary party shops in high streets, are also likely to be thick on the ground. Many of the more well established costumiers are already taking bookings. "Some of our members are anticipating hiring out their entire stock for the millennium and then retiring", says Peter Rigby of the British Costume Association, which represents 1000 shops throughout the UK. People seem to be looking at celebrating the last thousand years of history as a theme. Medieval and Victorian costumes are also likely to go down, as well as futuristic spacemen and alien costumes.

LEEDS: The city also has a regeneration programme, the **Millennium Square Project**.

LANCASTER: The City Council is creating a riverside park, the **River Lune Millennium Park**.

MERSEYSIDE AND HUMBERSIDE: A 714km **Trans Pennine Trail** will provide a route for walkers and cyclists linking Merseyside and Humberside.

PETERBOROUGH: Peterborough is building a **Green Wheel**, a new network of cycleways, footpaths and bridleways encircling the entire city. The wheel will link tourist attractions with nature reserves, picnic sites and sculpture trails, wildlife habitats and small parks. It will also feature three purpose-built heritage centres celebrating the city's culture, history and environment.

SHEFFIELD: A Millennium Gallery and Museum is to be built as part of Sheffield's **'Remaking the Heart of the City'** project, which will also include a covered **Winter Garden**.

STOKE-ON-TRENT: Ceramica will celebrate Staffordshire's famous pottery industry.

The 1999 total solar Eclipse

On the morning of Wednesday, August 11, 1999 large swathes of the northern hemisphere will experience one of the most spectacular solar eclipses for decades. The path of totality starts at sunrise in Nova Scotia and crosses northern France, southern

Belgium, Luxembourg, southern Germany, Austria, Hungary, northeastern Yugoslavia, Romania, northeastern Bulgaria, the Black Sea, central Turkey, northeastern Iraq, Iran, southern Pakistan, and central India, ending at sunset over the Bay of Bengal. A partial eclipse will be seen in countries from Greenland to Thailand.

In Britain the eclipse will be visible as a totality in a 100km wide strip encompassing Cornwall, western Devon, the Scilly Isles and Alderney in the Channel Islands; elsewhere in the UK the skies will darken measurably (London, for instance, will see a partial eclipse of 96 percent at around 11.20am). The last total eclipse in Britain was in June 1927, and the next is not due until 2090.

It will start to get dark around 10am: flowers will close up, birds will start nesting for the night, and the temperature will drop. Lasting for a maximum of two minutes and six seconds, the full eclipse goes into its total phase (known as 'second contact') at 11:11:15am over Cornwall. As totality occurs, the horizon will flame into orange and maroon hues as sunlight flashes through the lunar valleys on the eastern limb of the moon, creating a necklace of flaming bobs (known as Baily's Beads) around the moon's dark disc. The sun's corona will become visible as an irregular white ring around the moon, and thin arcs of gas should be visible streaming out from the solar poles. Planets such as Mercury and Venus, and stars (the brightest amongst them being Sirius, Regulus, Castor, Pollux and Procyon) will be easily visible. Full daylight will return at 12.30pm.

Comprehensive details on the eclipse are contained in a booklet, *A Guide to the 1999 Total Eclipse of the Sun*. It costs £5.95/US$10 (plus 50p postage, £1/US$1.63 overseas) from: The Royal Greenwich Observatory, Madingley Road, Cambridge CB3 OEZ ⓣ 01223/374000. The booklet includes a free 'eclipse viewer' made from aluminised mylar; these viewers are also available from Solar99, Belle Etoile, Rue du Hamel, Castel, Guernsey GY5 7QJ ⓣ 01481/64847 ⓕ 64871

ⓦ http:/www//visitbritain.com/millennium/ Official site of the British Tourist Authority, with news, events and attractions around Britain.

CORNWALL TRAVEL BRIEF

GETTING THERE The Cornwall Tourist Board advises visitors to stagger their journeys. Cornwall in peak season is prone to traffic jams anyway, and with 300,000 extra visitors, in addition to 250,000 peak-season visitors, it is very likely that roads may become gridlocked, especially around Lands End. Do not expect to be able to drive around much on the day. Extra trains will be running.

ACCOMMODATION Many hotels are already full. *The Land's End Hotel* had its first enquiries in 1991 and was fully booked by 1995; the *Queen's Hotel* in Penzance has been fully booked since early 1997. Emergency campsites are being prepared to cope with the influx. An accommodation guide is available from the tourist board.

PACKAGES A chartered train, the Millennium Eclipse Special, will leave London's Paddington station late on Tuesday night to arrive in Penzance on Wednesday morning, returning to London the same afternoon. Tickets will include a pre-departure party, on-board entertainment, champagne breakfast on arrival, and lunch. The Millennium Train Company Ⓣ 01737/223303. Ⓔ mtc2000@aol.com Ⓦ http://www.millennium.train.co.uk/

TOURIST OFFICES Cornwall Tourist Board, Daniell Road Centre, Lander Building, Daniell Road, Truro, Cornwall TR1 2DA Ⓣ 01872/274057.

SCOTLAND

Scotland's only Landmark Project is **Glasgow's Hampden Park Stadium**. The city is also hoping to build **X-Site**, a new national science centre which will include a planetarium, a millennium tower, and an IMAX cinema.

Edinburgh, scene of one of the country's biggest New Year's Eve parties (see box on p.97) is planning to transform a disused brewery in the old town into the city's first purpose-built visitor attraction, the **William Younger Centre**. Inside, a Dynamic Earth exhibition will trace the creation and evolution of life on the planet. Said to be the world's first geological visitor centre, its inspiration derives from the work of James Hutton, an eighteenth-century scientist described as the 'father of modern geology'. Themed areas within the centre will focus on the State of the Earth, with live links to volcanoes and earthquakes. Other geological phenomena – The Big Bang, Glaciation, Oceans, Polar and Mountain Zones, Grasslands, and the Tropics will also be featured. The £16 million (US$26m) centre is due to open in 1999.

In **Ayrshire** there are plans for the UK's first visitor centre devoted to invention and discovery. The Ardeer peninsula was the location of Alfred Noble's laboratory and chemicals company, and this particular connection has led to **The Big Idea**, which plans to celebrate Nobel, the Nobel Prize winners, and a thousand years of inventors, scientists and thinkers. Linked by the Millennium Bridge to Irvine harbourside, the centre will be a 'living laboratory for people who wish to think, to discover, to dream, to innovate and to invent'. If the funding comes through, work will start on the centre in spring 1998, ready for opening in the year 2000.

Scotland's colleges and research institutions are to be linked via the **University of the Highlands and Islands** and its history and culture made more widely available with the help of **SCRAN (The Scottish Cultural Resource Access Network)**. The project aims to digitise 1.5 million text records of historic monuments and artifacts held in museums and galleries, as well as a further 100,000 related archives which will be made available to schools, colleges and libraries throughout Scotland on CD-rom, the Internet and cable TV.

The country is also to have its own Millennium Wheel, but it is designed for transporting boats rather than for pleasure and forms part of the **Millennium Link**, a project to reopen navigation on the Firth & Clyde and the Union canals linking Glasgow and Edinburgh. The wheel will allow boats to transfer between the two canals at Falkirk, enabling freight or leisure boats to travel between the east and west coasts.

Hogmanay in Edinburgh

Scotland's Hogmanay traditions date back to the sixteenth century, when the Protestant fathers of the Kirk insisted that their followers treat Christmas Day as simply another working day because of its associations with Catholicism. New Year's Eve was judged a more favourable date for celebration, and eventually it grew to become an even bigger occasion than Christmas itself. The New Year's resolution, signifying a clean break with the past and a new beginning, is also firmly rooted in Hogmanay traditions.

Edinburgh's legendary New Year's Eve street parties grew spontaneously from their early beginnings, but the first official Hogmanay party took place in 1993, lasting three days and attracting a modest 50,000 revellers. Since then the annual celebration has grown at a phenomenal rate. In 1996 an estimated 300,000 people attended. Crowd density in Princes Street reached five people per square metre, leading to numerous cases of conjunctival haermorrhages, respiratory difficulties and panic attacks.

On New Year's Eve 1997 the city centre was barricaded off for safety reasons, with entrance by (free) Street Party passes restricted to 180,000 people. The emphasis shifted from 'the world's biggest street party' to 'one of the best New Year's Eve celebrations in the world'. The 1997/98 celebrations ran over four days, with over 50 events and 100 performance groups, and featured a torchlight procession and festival of fire, plays, concerts (both classical and rock), a children's Hogmanay, street theatre, and a street party with Salsa and Latin dance music.

Since 1996 Edinburgh's Hogmanay has been co-sponsored by the brewers Scottish & Newcastle and Richard Branson's Virgin group. The Virgin tycoon, a renowned party-lover, is determined to throw the 'party of the century' in Edinburgh which he hopes will outshine his arch-rival British Airways' sponsorship of the Millennium Experience at Greenwich.

Branson is also hoping to use the event to launch his latest balloon, a new airship called Millennia. Scheduled to depart from Edinburgh on New Year's Eve 1999, the Millennia will set off on a record-breaking world tour stopping in Greenwich, Paris, Moscow, Hong Kong and Sydney for Olympics 2000. The 248ft airship, capable of carrying up to 35 passengers, is being built by the Lightship Group, a joint venture between Virgin and the American Blimp Corporation of Oregon. With an envelope volume of around 500,000 cubic feet, it will be larger than any airship currently flying, and it will cruise at 60 miles an hour on non-stop flights of up to 3000 miles.

Edinburgh and Lothians Tourist Board, 3 Princes Street, Edinburgh
℗ 0131/ 557 1700.

Glasgow: National Stadium

The home of Queen's Park Rangers, Glasgow's **Hampden Park Stadium** is being rebuilt to international standards. The £46 million (US$75m) project will include a new South

Stand, a Museum of Football, an international media centre, and sports research facilities. The stadium is due to open autumn 1999.

National Stadium, Hampden Park, Mount Florida, Glasgow G42 9DA
Ⓣ 0141/636 1390 Ⓕ 636 6087.

Global Telethon

The Glasgow-based Millennial Foundation is promoting a global telethon, the world's largest fundraising event ever, which it hopes will raise up to £500 million (US$815m) for the charity Yes 2000 (Youth and Environmental Support for the Year 2000). With the support of UNESCO, the foundation is planning a series of televised, fundraising parties spanning 31 cities in 24 time zones, starting in Fiji and winding up in the Cook Islands. Yes 2000 will also include a series of special events and exhibitions to be held worldwide during 1999 and 2000.

The Millennial Foundation, 10 Sandyford Place, Glasgow G3 7NB
Ⓣ 0141/ 204 2000 Ⓕ 248 1591.

WALES

Wales's sole Landmark Project is Cardiff's **Millennium Stadium**, although the city will also acquire the **Wales Millennium Centre**, a multipurpose arts, entertainment and education centre featuring exhibition galleries, an **IMAX** cinema, a lyric theatre, public piazzas, and other facilities.

In Carmarthenshire the Regency park of Middleton Hall is being transformed into the **National Botanic Garden of Wales**, which will feature woodland, terraced, alpine and rock gardens, biomass plantations, and water and wetland gardens with the most extensive collection of aquatic plants in Europe.

Cardiff: Millennium Stadium

Cardiff's new 75,000-seater stadium at Cardiff Arms Park will have a retractable roof for all-weather use and will also feature a Rugby Experience museum. The £144 million (US$234m) project will be completed in time to host the Rugby World Cup in 1999.

Millennium Stadium, St David's House, 1st floor, west wing, Wood Street, Cardiff CF1 1EF ⓣ 01222/232 661.

COUNTRY CODE ⓣ 44

CANADA

T he forward-thinking Canadians began planning for the millennium more than two decades ago and, indeed, the country has nurtured 'future studies' and futuristic thinkers since the **Muskoka Institute for the Future** was founded in the 1970s. During that decade it held a series of conferences on future directions for humanity at a time when silicon chips and satellite communications were just appearing on the world stage. **The World Future Society** met in Toronto in 1980, attracting 6000 participants, the same year that futurist Don Toppin founded **Toronto/2000**. The **World Millennium Network** was founded in 1986. A decade later and the **Millennium Council of Canada** came into being, an umbrella organisation representing the many different millennial programmes in the country.

In September 1997 the Canadian government launched its own initiatives. "It will be an unequalled opportunity to show ourselves and the world the richness of our diversity, the strength of Canadian values, and the great promise of our future in the twenty-first century", said Prime Minister Jean Chretien. One of the government's primary commitments is to a **Millennium Scholarship Fund** which will help low-to moderate-income students 'prepare for the knowledge-based society of the next century'. A **Millennium Task Force** has also been set up whose aim is to establish a national framework between government departments, the private sector, and non-governmental bodies for the celebrations.

Canada has numerous programmes operating at community level. The bigger, international-scale celebrations are likely to take place in cities such as **Vancouver** and **Toronto**.

Millennium Council of Canada, 11th floor, East Tower, Toronto City Hall, 100 Queen Street West, Toronto, Ontario M5H 2N2 Ⓣ 416/392 129 Ⓕ 392 1289 Ⓔ grtmill@idirect.com Ⓦ http://www.2000.ca

Canadian Millennium Ⓦ http://www.2000cdn.com
An excellent site which came on-line in 1998 containing links to all the main projects in each Canadian province, government programmes, and tourism information.

Events

Bobcaygeon 2000

This small Ontario village of 2500 people has initiated several projects to mark the millennium, including developing a health care plan (Wellness 2000), refurbishing their retail area, and inviting local schools to create a Peace Park.

Team Bobcaygeon 2000, PO Box 125, Bobcaygeon, Ontario KOM 1AU Ⓣ 705/738 9100 Ⓕ 738 1721.

Calgary 2000

This organisation is developing themes and initiatives for celebrating the millennium in conjunction with community

associations, schools, arts and entertainment groups and local businesses.

Calgary 2000, #2000, PO Box 2100, Station M, Calgary, Alberta T2P 2M5
Ⓣ 403/268 2000 Ⓕ 268 5245 Ⓔ istime@cadvision.com
Ⓦ http://www.intervisual.com/calgary2000/

Community Enrichment Foundation

The foundation aims to foster community-based wealth and social well-being. Programmes for the millennium include Health Care 2000 and Education 2000.

Community Enrichment Foundation, 5460 Yonge Street #602, North York, Ontario M2N 6K7 Ⓣ 416/733 9735 Ⓕ 733 4560 Ⓔ rayvafa@ftn.net

Community Project Centre of Canada

The millennium project 'Canada Cares' focuses on a campaign to have the United Nations declare Canada the safest country in the world by the year 2000.

Community Project Centre of Canada, Flat Iron building, 49 Wellington
Avenue East, Toronto, Ontario M5E 1C9 Ⓣ 416/367 245 Ⓕ 866 2941.

Halifax 2000

Celebrations will focus on the cultural, ethnic and historical
realities of Halifax and Dartmouth, as well as on the 250-year
anniversaries of their founding.

Halifax 2000, c/o Tourism, Culture and Heritage Division, PO Box 1749,
Halifax, N.S. B3J 3A5 Ⓣ 902/420 4724 Ⓕ 490 5950.

International Foundation of Learning

'Education for Global Citizenship' is a project intended to
foster the development of global citizenship among the youth
of British Colombia.

International Foundation of Learning, #209 1628 West 1st Avenue,
Vancouver, BC V6J 1G1 Ⓣ 604/734 2544 Ⓕ 734 9723
Ⓔ desgerri@direct.ca

Millennium Community Building Association

The MCBA aims to create new ways of helping older people
remain in their communities by providing safe, accessible
housing alternatives.

MCBA, The Catalyst, 712 Hillsdale Avenue East, Toronto, Ontario M4S 1V3
Ⓣ 416/487 2251 Ⓕ 487 5616 Ⓔ pjwade@The Catalyst.com

Millennium Council of Newfoundland & Labrador

The year 2000 will mark the 1000-year anniversary of the
establishment of the first Viking settlement in the New World
at L'Anse aux Meadows on the Great Northern Peninsula of

Newfoundland. There will be a **Viking 1000 Snowmobile Race**, which takes participants through the L'Anse aux Meadows World Heritage Area, and also Viking festivals in nearby communities. **Cape Spear**, the most easterly point on the Avalon Peninsula, will be the first place to see the dawn of the new millennium on the North American continent.

Millennium Council of Newfoundland & Labrador, 8 Appledore Place, St John's, Newfoundland A1B 2W9 ⓉＴ 709/722 4003 Ⓕ 722 4003.

Millennium Eve Vigil

This project aims to create 'a significant 24-hour context in which to celebrate the turn of the millennium with friends, family and community' by holding a vigil that will allow people to examine their past, look at the present and imagine the future.

Millennium Eve Vigil, 2 Slade Avenue, Toronto M6G 3A1 Ⓣ 416/653 0563 Ⓦ http://www.hcol.humberc.on.ca/html/milvigil/index.HTM

Millennium Foundation of Canada

Claiming to be the 'first organisation in the world dedicated solely to the creation of legacies to mark the year 2000', the foundation is the home of the **Earth Legacies** project and **Wills for the Earth**, which encourages people to leave legacies in their wills to help fund recognised environmental organisations of their choice.

The Millennium Foundation of Canada, 330 East 7th Avenue, Suite 104, Vancouver, BC, V5T 4K5 Ⓣ 604/708 3474 Ⓔ nvbentum@cyberstore.ca Ⓦ http://www.millennia.org/

Millennium Vancouver 2000!

This consortium of business, arts, community and government leaders is planning an international-scale celebration for Vancouver. Plans include the **MV2000! Citizens Legacy** (educational projects and a time capsule), an **MV2000! Financial**

Legacy (an endowment fund for the arts and community projects), **MV2000! Community Partners** (community arts groups and other organisations developing events), **MV2000! International Partnerships** (linking up with other celebrations, including joint satellite links on New Year's Eve 1999), and the **MV2000! Secretariat** (helping other communities in British Columbia plan their celebrations). Some events being planned include a Time Festival and a Futurists Festival.

Millennium Vancouver 2000!, PO Box 48381, 595 Burrard Street, Bentall Centre, Vancouver BC, V7X 1A2 ⓣ 604/618 5825 ⓕ 684 6888 ⓔ millennium@vancouver2000.bc.ca

Music Canada 2000

'A musical festival and display of Canadian artistic and cultural resources on a scale never attempted before', **Music Canada 2000** will bring together composers, musicians and performers from all over the country for a concentrated period of activities honoring Canadian achievements past and present.

Music Canada 2000, 67 Woodlawn Avenue West, Toronto, Ontario M4V 1G6 ⓣ 416/397 5727 ⓕ 392 3355.

Toronto 2000

Toronto 2000 – An Urban Odyssey is a series of celebrations, events and activities covering areas such as culture, sports and education. Plans are also being developed for gala New Year's Eve celebrations, a major urban summit and an Exposition of the Future which will operate over six months.

Toronto 2000, 1 Yonge Street, Suite 2000, Toronto, Ontario M5E 1N4 ⓣ 416/777 2000 ⓕ 862 8111 ⓔ mjadpr2@inforamp.net

Turning 2000 Project

The project is offering CAN$2,000 (£855/US$1400) in prizes and seed money to local projects 'for the best ideas to make the world a better place in the new millennium'. Organisers are looking for 2000 suggestions to start the millennium off on the right foot, and have gone into partnership with a charitable society to collect donations from businesses and individuals to help seed and encourage local projects with sustainable goals.

Turning 2000 Project, Box 175, Station A, Ottawa, Ontario K1N 8V2 Ⓕ 613/ 562 4055 Ⓦ http://www.turning2000.org/

Winnipeg Millennium Committee

Projects range from a major expansion of Winnipeg's library to helping school children record their family trees.

Winnipeg Millennium Committee, 124 Rue St Pierre, Winnipeg, Manitoba R3V 1J8 Ⓣ 204/957 2820 Ⓕ 943 2261 Ⓔ wholewen@telpay.ca

International Projects

Beacon Millennium

Canada is part of the global Beacon Millennium Project (see section on Britain, p.57). Beacons of all kinds will be lit, sweeping across time zones from St John's and Halifax to Vancouver and Victoria.

Beacon Millennium (Canada), 132 Medland Street, Toronto, Ontario M6P 2N5
Ⓣ 416/766 675 Ⓕ 766 9675.

Canadian Foundation for World Development

The CFWD has been in existence for over twenty years and runs 'People to People' self-help programmes which send volunteers to developing countries. Millennium projects include a 'sweating hose irrigation system', enabling farmers to grow several crops in a season, and a three-bedroom plastic house which can be assembled in 24 hours with just a screwdriver.

CFWD, 2441 Bayview Avenue, Willowdale, Ontario M2L 1A5 Ⓣ 416/445 474
Ⓕ 441 4025.

Global Foundation for Understanding

The foundation is planning a 'Great Millennium Campaign', which will include a series of events and activities emphasising the universal languages of art, imagery and music. There will also be a global singalong of 'Great Millennium Songs' in all 24 times zones at 12 noon on January 1, 2000.

Global Foundation for Understanding, 4th floor, 49 Wellington Street East,
Toronto, Ontario M5E 1CP Ⓣ 905/881 2000 Ⓕ 630 1805
Ⓔ grtmill@idirect.com

i human 2000

This organisation intends to ask distinguished politicians, scientists, poets, philosophers and religious leaders to identify the most important event or influence to affect humanity in the last 1000 years and the next 100 years. It will then create a series of artworks based on these themes which, it is hoped, will form a touring exhibition to major art galleries in the world. Organisers also plan to invite 200 children from around the world to create a sculpture.

i human 2000, 11241 - 78 Avenue, Edmonton, Alberta T6G OM8
Ⓣ 403/435 7646 Ⓕ 433 4755.

International School Peace Gardens

Organised by the International Holistic Tourism Education Centre (IHEC), the **International School Peace Gardens** project aims to help schools in Canada, Australia, Mexico and elsewhere in the world create a Peace Garden, Peace Tree or Peace Grove for the year 2000. Around 400 schools so far.

IHEC, 3342 Masthead Crescent, Mississauga, Ontario L5L 1G9
Ⓣ / Ⓕ 905/ 820 5067 Ⓔ jmarr@utcc.utronoto.ca

Ronde et Bleue

This Quebec city group plans to create a 'planetary choir' singing the 'Peace Hymn' to welcome in the year 2000. The choir will comprise as many people on earth as possible, 'united in the same vibration and singing at exactly the same time, at the same tempo and the same pitch, with each participant singing in their own language'.

Ronde et Bleue Ⓣ 418/651 6039 Ⓕ 651 4186.

Rhythm of the Earth

More global drumming (see also Britain and Boston), with a plan for people to celebrate midnight in each time zone through drumming in order 'to make the earth reverberate in unison as part of a global drumfest'.

Rhythm of the Earth, Ⓔ bhdrum@vaxxine.com
Ⓦ http://www.vaxxine.com/bhdrum/

Welcome 2000/Bienvenue 2000

A project of the **Year 2000 World Festivities Project** of Montreal, the main aim of **Welcome 2000** is to develop a series of activities around the world to celebrate the millennium, with a 24-hour televisual programme which will be broadcast onto a giant screen at each local event.

Year 2000 Festivities Corporation, 100 Des Ormes, Vaudreuil-sur-le-lac, Quebec J7V 8P3 Ⓣ 514/862 2823 Ⓕ 688 7038 Ⓔ ppatry@telug.uquebec.ca

TRAVEL BRIEF

Many families are likely to take the opportunity to stage big reunions at the millennium, and with large numbers of people from the US, Europe and Asia flocking in to Canada to visit relatives flights may fill up fast.

GETTING THERE Book sensibly over peak holiday periods.

ACCOMMODATION Accommodation in Vancouver and Toronto may be in short supply and, as everywhere, the better hotels nationwide are laying on their own celebration packages. Canadian Pacific, who own 27 of the country's finest landmark hotels, are currently running waiting lists while they work out the fine points of their individual programmes.

Central booking for Canada and the US: Ⓣ 800/441 1414. UK: Ⓣ 0500/303 030. Unusual celebrations such as the 1000-year anniversary of the Viking landings in Newfoundland are likely to be heavily booked well in advance.

TOURIST OFFICES There is no national tourist office; each province has its own headquarters in the state capital. Amongst these are: Ontario: Queen's Park, Toronto, Ontario M7A 2E5 Ⓣ 800/668 2746; Quebec: Tour de la Place Victoria, Bureau 260, Montreal, Quebec H4Z 1C3 Ⓣ 514/873 7977 or 800/363 7777; British Columbia: Parliament Building, Victoria, British Columbia V8V 1X4 Ⓣ 800/663 6000; Alberta: 3rd Floor, 10155 102nd St, Edmonton, Alberta T31 4L6 Ⓣ 800/661 8888. UK: London Ⓣ 0891/715 000 (premium rate). US: the toll-free numbers quoted for the provincial offices can be dialled from anywhere within North America. Ⓦ http://info.ic.gc.ca/Tourism/

COUNTRY CODE Ⓣ 1

EGYPT

T he Great Pyramids at Giza are destined to be one of the most popular locations for organisers of multizone millennium parties around the world, not to mention all the mystics and prophets who venerate the ancient stones. For many years the **Millennium Society** has been promoting 'the biggest party in the world on December 31, 1999, at the Great Pyramids', and more recently the US-based **Billennium Organizing Committee** has added the Pyramids to its list of party locations. But the question is still being asked – who, exactly, is going to be there?

Will these rival groups spoil the occasion by jostling for space beneath the gaze of the Sphinx? Mark Mitten, president of the Billennium Organising Committee, has dismissed such allegations, stating that his committee has now been approached by the Millennium Society with an offer to work together on the celebrations. "There are several groups attempting to lay claim to the Pyramids", he adds. "We our-

selves have been offered a location at the site but we remain cautious about exactly what can be done at the site and how many people/groups will be overseeing the celebrations."

The Egyptian Tourist Authority, rather belatedly realising the potential of their most popular tourist attraction, stated in late 1997 that "we have decided that the Pyramids at Giza is the perfect place to celebrate the birth of the millennium, and we have confirmed that there will be some kind of celebration at this location." The Tourist Authority is still deciding which group to choose, however, but one thing is certain – if you're planning New Year's Eve here, it will be a dry celebration. No alcohol can be consumed on site.

Finally, if you're absolutely desperate to watch the sun rise over the Pyramids, a recent independent travellers' newsletter reports that this is possible from a hill overlooking the City of the Dead, provided the appropriate *baksheesh* is paid to the police on site.

TRAVEL BRIEF

Although it appears that there will be something happening at the Pyramids, no one can yet advise on travel plans. As a general rule Egypt is a difficult destination for the independent traveller and it is usually easier and cheaper to join up with a package tour operator. The only tour operator with access rights to date is Abercrombie & Kent, who are planning a 'small gathering' at the Pyramids as part of a New Year's Eve weekend package.

GETTING THERE There are regular scheduled flights to Cairo from many places in Europe and Africa, and more limited options from the US. Mid-winter is high season and flights are often full over Christmas and the New Year.

ACCOMMODATION The major cities have a good range of luxury hotels, but any spare rooms will be filled up with celebrating locals, so book in advance. Good mid-range and cheap hotels are hard to find in Egypt at the best of times.

TOURIST OFFICES CAIRO: 5 Adly St, Cairo Ⓣ 02/391 3454. Also at the airport, railway station, and opposite the Mena House Hotel, Giza. UK: London Ⓣ 0171/493 5282. US: New York Ⓣ 212/332 2570; Los Angeles Ⓣ 213/653 8815; Chicago Ⓣ 312/280 4666 Ⓦ http://touregypt.net/

COUNTRY CODE Ⓣ 20

FINLAND

R ecent scientific research on the increased activity of sunspots seems to indicate that during the year 2000 we will witness some of the most spectacular manifestations of the Northern Lights ever seen. One of the best places to watch the Aurora Borealis is Lapland, but elsewhere in Finland they have devised their own way of illuminating the dark, five-month-long winter.

Helsinki

Inaugurated in 1995, Helsinki's **Festival of Light**, or Valon Voimat (which translates as 'the forces of light'), builds on existing Finnish traditions (such as placing lighted candles in windows on December 6, Independence Day) and features creations of light and sound performances by artists throughout the city, illuminations of buildings, and a Light Fair. The Festival of Light, 'which draws its power from darkness', is developing spectacular displays for 1999 and 2000. It will be open between November and December.

Helsinki is also one of the nine **European Cities of Culture 2000**, with the theme of '**Knowledge, Technology and the Future**'. Nearly 300 million Finnish marks (£34m/US$56m) are being invested in an international cultural programme that will include dance, visual arts, opera, ballet, musicals, rock and jazz, as well as sports, equestrian events and a **Tall Ships** festival. The city has recently built a new **Opera House** and the 14,000-seat **Arena Show Hall**. The year 2000 will also mark the completion of a new **Museum of Modern**

Art, the **Ethnographic Museum**, and a **Media Centre**. During 1999 Finland presides over the EU, and in December 1999 the capital will host the **EU Summit**. The year 2000 also marks the 450-year anniversary of the founding of the city.

Helsinki Festival: August 20–September 5 1999; August 25–September 10 2000 Ⓣ 09/135 4522; Festival of Light, Fredrikinkatu 61a, 00100 Helsinki, Finland Ⓣ 50 552 9272 Ⓕ 605 297 Ⓔ info@mail.festivals.fi

Helsinki 2000, Eteläranta 16 00130 Helsinki, Finland Ⓣ 09/169 32 11 Ⓕ 169 32 04 Ⓔ info@2000.hel.fi

Ⓦ http://www.nls.fi/ptk/positio/uutisia/pos96108.html

Ⓦ http://www.minedu.fi/tkt/eu/hki2000.html (both in Finnish only).

Helsinki's Virtual Reality Dream

With winter in Finland lasting anything up to 200 days, and average temperatures in January plummeting as low as -30°C, it's hardly surprising that many Finns prefer to let their keyboards do the walking. The country has one of the highest per capita uses of the Internet in the world, and it's estimated that around 60 percent of the five million population are connected to it. By the year 2000, the residents of Helsinki won't have to venture out of doors at all if they so choose. In the biggest experiment of its kind in the world, 100,000 people are being wired into a virtual city which will allow them to see plays and concerts, go shopping, drop in on musicians performing in the central square, attend university lectures, meet the bank manager, visit friends for a chat and much more besides – all with real-time video links.

The project, **Helsinki Arena 2000**, involves creating a 3-D model (VRML) of the city detailing all its streets, shopping areas, cultural institutions, businesses and Government offices, which will then be linked via telephone, broadband and Internet networks to an integrated package easily accessible from home PCs. Small video cameras can be hooked up to

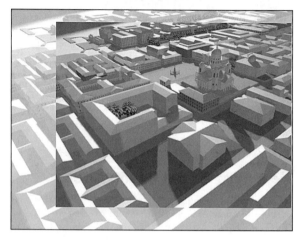

PCs to provide real-time video and sound links. New network technology will also enable Internet calls to be dialled on a conventional phone line. Whilst strolling around the virtual city, it will be possible to simply click on a shop or business and be connected via a normal telephone.

The brainchild of computer engineer Risto Linturi, the project is being financed by the **Helsinki Telephone Company** in collaboration with local universities, banks, newspapers, cable TV companies, the City of Helsinki and companies such as Nokia, IBM and ICL. "I've read about a thousand sci-fi novels and have never come across an idea like this", says Risto. "I'm very proud of it. One of the most important things in this project for me is that it enables anyone to transmit their own video programmes into the network at the same cost as making an ordinary call, and much more easily than setting up your own Web pages", he says.

The Finns' answer to Bill Gates, Risto Linturi works himself from a purpose-built home on the edge of the Baltic Sea, teleconferencing via large screens with his work colleagues in the city.

The technical background to the project is available at
Ⓦ http://www.helsinkiarena2000.fi/summary/

If you have the appropriate VRML plug-ins you can also see a demonstration of Helsinki's 3D phone book at:
Ⓦ http://www.helsinkiarena2000.fi/summary/demos.html

TRAVEL BRIEF

Beautiful, bleak, chilly Finland is not usually high on the list of holiday hotspots, except over Christmas and New Year. Sensible booking precautions should give you the arrangements you want in the year 2000.

GETTING THERE Finnair has 42 flights a week from the UK, one daily flight from New York (with possible other US departure cities in summer). Although Helsinki is Finland's only major international airport, air travel is popular and convenient inside the country, with a tightly packed schedule of domestic services among 22 cities and with reasonably priced airpasses. There are good rail services between all major towns as well as links to neighbouring countries. Scandinavian Seaways and Silja Line jointly operate ferry connections with the UK via Gothenburg in Sweden.

ACCOMMODATION Much of Finland's tourist accommodation is geared to winter sports and summer lakes, with small country hotels and cottages. Helsinki does have a number of larger hotels, but advance booking is recommended.

TOURIST OFFICES National: Eteläesplanadi 4, FIN-00130 Helsinki Ⓣ 09/4176 9300 Ⓕ 4176 9301; Helsinki: Pohjoisesplanadi 19, FIN-00100, Helsinki Ⓣ 09/169 3757 Ⓕ 169 3839. UK: London Ⓣ 0171/839 4048. US: New York Ⓣ 212/370 5540 Ⓦ http://www.hel.fi/english

COUNTRY CODE Ⓣ 358

FRANCE

T he French have been slow on the uptake for celebrating the approaching millennium, shrugging off the idea with typical Gallic insouciance until it was almost too late to do anything. The idea is "not particularly French", said one official.

But the feverish activity in other European countries touched a raw nerve and, not wanting to be left behind, on April 4, 1997 (the start of the 1000-day countdown to the year 2000) the French government unveiled its own master plan, the **Mission for the Celebration of the Year 2000**, with the slogan, 'In 2000, France, Europe, the World, a New Inspiration'. Proposing a calendar of new events to 'celebrate, share and think over themes such as nature, knowledge, innovation and solidarity', the Mission is intended to reflect France's role in the formulation of the 'universal values' arising from the Enlightenment.

The Mission's plans involve an '**enterprise club**' and a **think-tank**, both of which will be used as a forum for the exchange of ideas with philosophers, social scientists, writers and other prominent personalities. At the suggestion of the think-tank, 27 issues for the twenty-first century will be the subject of 27 conferences to take place in the French regions, departments and overseas territories. The first of these took place in Lyon in October 1997, and the last will be in Reims on August 10, 1999, during the last solar eclipse of the millennium.

The Mission also announced a round-the-world millennial sailboat race, dubbed '**La Course – The Race**', which will depart from Marseille on December 31, 2000.

Many provincial cities have announced plans for events and exhibitions in 1999 and 2000, including Avignon, which is to be one of nine European Cities of Culture 2000.

Other non-official plans underway include architect Paul Chemetov's project for a **Giant Hedge** stretching from Calais to Carcassonne and the creation of **Generation 2000**, an organisation aimed at those born in 1980 who will be 20 years old at the millennium. Already claiming 30,000 members, the club aims to have a grand reunion on New Year's Eve and exchange visits with other 20-year-olds around the world, and plans to launch two magazines whose unique selling point will be that they grow old at the same time as their readers...the two magazines have been given the names, strangely, of 'Kevin' and 'Ophélie'.

Mission pour la célébration de l'an 2000, 36 rue Lacépède, 75005 Paris
Ⓣ 01/53 71 20 00 Ⓕ 53 71 20 01 Ⓔ dircom@celebration.2000.gouv.fr
Ⓦ http://www.celebration2000.gouv.fr
Ⓦ http://www.celebration2000.gouv.fr/uk/htm/
Bilingual site detailing the French government's plans for the Year 2000, including information on how to participate in the 27 regional discussion forums on millennial themes.
Ⓦ http://www.tour-eiffel.fr/teiffel/an2000_uk/
From the top of the Eiffel Tower, an overview of the year 2000 and its history and future. Bilingual French and English.

Paris

Paris has also been spurred into action relatively recently. At the launch of **Paris 2000** its president, Yves Morousi, said that the city should take its part in the "international competition which the Year 2000 has created between the capitals of the world", adding that "we have to try and recapture the spirit of the City of Light which, in 1900, led the world on the occasion of the Universal Exhibition."

Spurred on by traditional rivalries with *les rosbifs* over the Channel, the French announced a millennium Ferris wheel that would be 'bigger and better' than London's Millennium Wheel – and twice as expensive. The designer of the project stated that "if necessary, we will just go one metre higher" in order to beat their 500ft-high London rival.

Nothing has been heard of the wheel since, although in December 1997 the French announced a shortlist of lavish and fairly bizarre gestures that will include the Eiffel Tower laying a giant luminous egg, shoals of multicoloured plastic fish swarming in the Seine (which will be perfumed for the event) and a new wooden tower rising up 650ft on the banks of the river. "From today, we are a length ahead of the rest of the world", said Morousi.

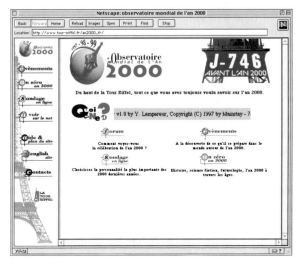

The French press begged to disagree, pouring scorn on the dramatic and controversial plan to turn the Eiffel Tower into a hi-tech chicken for a night. At 11pm on December 21, 1999, an enormous egg will descend out of the belly of the tower, to the sound of 2000 drums from five continents. At midnight, the egg will crack open to reveal hundreds of television screens relaying images of millennium parties from around the globe. *Le Figaro* described the idea as 'ridiculous', whilst other critics wondered if perhaps the organiser would be giving birth to a turkey rather than a hi-tech egg.

The Eiffel Tower has its own millennium countdown clock, a giant installation 33m across which weighs 50 tonnes and features 1342 spotlights. But the first ever millennium clock built in this era, the celebrated **Génitron**, has come unstuck. This huge sculpture unveiled with great pomp by President Mitterand on January 31, 1987, when it began counting down from 450 million seconds outside the Pompidou Centre, was unfortunately taken away in August 1996 when renovation work began on the centre. There are no plans to restore it, according to one of the designers, François Scali, who is suing the museum to try and get it reinstated. "The space which was occupied by the Génitron will become a transit zone as part of the redesign", said the director of the centre, Jean-Jacques Aillagon. Ironically, M. Aillagon is also chairman of Mission 2000, the official government body overseeing the millennium celebrations.

The permanent architectural centrepiece of Paris's celebrations is to be a 650ft-high **Tour de la Terre** (The Earth Tower), to be built alongside the Seine in the city's eastern districts at a cost of Ffr. 247 million (£25m/US$41m). The tower will include a 3000-square-metre raised platform with bars, restaurants and exhibition areas. "Paris will once more be asserting its modernity by offering the world the Tour de la Terre, a permanent reminder of its message to preserve the planet", said Morousi. French ecology groups were quick to point out the hypocrisy of an environmental symbol that might be built from tropical hardwoods, but the designers say that it will be built mostly from common pine.

Other plans that have been unveiled include the conversion of the **Place de la Concorde** into a giant sundial, using the Egyptian obelisk at its centre as a pointer, and turning the **Place Charles de Gaulle Etoile** into a giant clock, using powerful lights mounted on the **Arc de Triomphe** to countdown to 2000 on the twelve avenues leading into the square. Outside the **Hôtel de Ville** there will also be a giant electronic book, 22m wide and 15m high, which will offer a different theme on French literature on a daily basis, allowing passersby to browse through 170 acres of prose during the course of the year.

In the **Seine**, 2000 brightly coloured plastic fish will stick out 10ft from the water as 'symbols of the vitality of the city and witnesses to its future'. The real fish in the river may not have a future to witness, since leading French scent manufacturers are planning to perfume its waters for the millennium.

At the **Longchamps racecourse** there will be a concert in homage to Jimi Hendrix, marking thirty years since Woodstock, and there are also plans to turn Paris's ring road, the boulevard périphérique, into a vast concert venue for New Year's Eve, with every type of music being performed on stages around its length.

Full details on Paris events were due to have been announced in April 1998.

Paris 2000, 32 quai des Celestins, 75004 Paris ℗ 01/42 76 73 90.

Events

Paris: Cité des Sciences

1999

The overall theme of this project will be 'New Ways of Learning and Inventing', demonstrating how communications technology is changing the relationship between knowledge and people in the spheres of culture, sciences, research, education and work.

2000–2001

Exhibitions will revolve around two themes – 'The Living' and 'The Environment' – and explore the changing inter-relationships between humans, the environment and the planet.

Running out of Fizz?

With millions of people expected to toast the arrival of the new millennium, the viticulturalists of France's Champagne region are already experiencing a boom in sales. But the question is now being asked whether there will be enough to go around?

Many people have already started to lay down vintage bottles ready for the year 2000, and the Champagne houses have warned that the cellars will be empty by the millennium. Top bubbly, which will be at its peak in 1999, is selling fast, and experts predict that prices will soar as demand increases. Certain vintages (Bollinger RD 1985, Veuve Cliquot 1990 and Roederer Cristal 1989) have already sold out.

The champagne shortage is little more than a myth, however, propagated to a large degree by dishonest merchants trying to flog 'millennium champagne' by the caseload. A strong possibility exists that champagne producers may yet declare another vintage, which will alleviate shortages and further boost their profits.

If you're not too fussy about what you guzzle, there is really no need to panic. Non-vintages are unlikely to run out. Current stocks stand at around one billion bottles, with around 250 million more being produced every year. World demand is presently around 246 million bottles annually, so even if you leave your visit to the wine shop until the afternoon of December 31, 1999, there will still be plenty of non-vintage (and perhaps even some vintage) champagnes to buy. Good years to look out for include 1985, 1988, 1989, 1990, 1995 and 1996.

Le Parc et la Grande Halle de la Villette

Mid-September to mid-November, 1999

This special event includes a unique production of the annual *Rencontres Urbain* festival with original works in dance, music, theatre, writing, cinema and audiovisual arts.

2000

An exhibition on 'Man and Conflict' will pose the question – 'why war?', moving on to explore 'how to avoid war' through four or five typical war scenarios. Alongside the exhibition there will be debates, films, talks, and music on the same theme.

June 2000

A special edition of the annual fireworks festival in the **Parc de la Villette** will be held for two nights, with link-ups to similar events in Buenos Aires, Tokyo and elsewhere. Around 40,000 people usually attend.

Les Galeries Nationales du Grand Palais

Autumn 1999

'France in the Year 1000' is the subject of this exhibit. Art and civilisation in France from the end of the ninth to the second half of the eleventh century will be explored, including the 'terrors' of the year 1000.

2000

'Visions of the Future' is a display centred on historical representations of the future with works selected from international collections.

Le Palais du Cinema

December 1999

This month will see the opening of the new **Palais des Arts du Cinema** in the Palais du Tokyo (avenue du Pt Wilson).

2000

A film festival will take place throughout the year focusing on the theme of 'civilisation and the cinema'.

Avignon: Summer Festival

Mid-July to mid-August 2000

Avignon's theme as one of the European Cities of Culture 2000 is the 'Theatre of the World'. Avignon's summer theatre festival is one of the largest in the world, attracting 120,000 spectators for a month-long extravaganza of the performing arts. In 2000 the festival will be marked by major performances in the Court of Honour in the **Palace of the Popes** as well, involving theatre companies from Eastern Europe under the programme 'Theatres of the East and West – European Millennial Encounters'. Avignon is also planning to create a fabulous garden, covering 80 acres, between its new TGV station and the city's medieval ramparts where a **Festival of Gardens** on an island in the Durance will be held in collaboration with landscape artists from the eight other cultural capitals.

Mission Avignon 2000, Hotel de Ville, 84045 Avignon
Ⓣ 04/90 80 80 00 Ⓕ 90 80 82 82.

Blois 2000: Wonder and Enchantment

A series of events are planned on the theme of 'Wonder and Enchantment', with historical figures (Leonardo da Vinci, Nostradamus, François I) acting as guides. The surrounding forests will be populated by wondrous animals and figures from forest fables. A magic garden will link the château to the House of Magic.

Bordeaux 2000: La Triennale

The renovation of the city's monuments and tramway will be celebrated in a major architecture exhibition, **La Triennale**. A major exhibition devoted to local and worldwide winemaking will also be held.

La Course – The Race

Conceived by navigator Bruno Peyron (first winner of the Jules Verne trophy for sailing around the world in less than eighty days), the race is intended to encourage technological innovation, since there are no restrictions on the types of boats competing, and naval architects and sailors will be free to create 'the vessels of the twenty-first century'. Sixty seven candidates from seventeen countries have applied to take part.

Bruno Peyron's maxicatamaran *Explorer* will promote the race as it attempts various record-breaking challenges on the world's oceans between now and the year 2000. Schools, universities, and community organisations in France have also been invited to participate via live satellite links, enabling them to explore the scientific, oceanographic and cultural dimensions of *Explorer's* voyages.

La Course – The Race, Mer & Media, 55 blvd d'Armorique, 357000 Rennes, France Ⓣ 02/99 84 64 64 Ⓕ 99 84 64 65
Ⓦ http://www.therace.org

Brest 2000: La Course – The Race

Brest will be one of the official departure points for **The Race – La Course** (see box above). It is also planning its own regatta of 2000 boats on January 1, 2000. A major maritime film festival is also scheduled.

Nantes 2000: Festival of the Four Continents

Nantes' annual Festival of the Four Continents will be enlarged to include new countries. It will take place between the last weekend of 1999 and the first weekend of 2000. Several exhibitions centred on **Jules Verne**, who was born in the city, are to be held, including one on the theme 'Jules Verne, futurism and imaginary utopias'.

Strasbourg: Festival of Theatre

1999–2000

The city's theme for the millennium is 'Links' – between the past and the future, between countries, and between people. There will be a special **Festival of Theatre** (end of September to Christmas 1999), a celebration of the pont de l'Europe, and an exhibition on links between the past and the future through the art of divination.

Toulouse 2000: Sky and Space

The aeronautically oriented city of Toulouse is holding several exhibitions on the theme of **Sky and Space**. The newly opened **Cité de l'Espace** will host a major programme with links to other space centres worldwide and an international convention on space law. Events at the **Musée de l'Aeronautique** revolve around the Conquest of the Skies, and the **Musée d'Art Moderne** and the **Musée des Beaux-Arts** will jointly host an exhibition on Space in the Plastic Arts.

TRAVEL BRIEF

The busiest events in France are likely to be New Year's Eve in Paris and the Avignon Festival in 2000. Throughout the summer, there are hundreds and thousands of small, entertaining cultural festivals in every country town and hamlet, most of them adding a millennial touch in 2000.

GETTING THERE It is always worth booking ahead over holiday periods. The nearest international airport for Avignon is Marseilles; Avignon will also have a new TGV station in time for the festival.

ACCOMMODATION Accommodation will be tight in Paris for New Year's Eve 1999, with the great palace hotels such as the George V and the Crillon already running long waiting lists. Book at least six months ahead for the Avignon Festival. Look also at hotels in Arles, St-Rémy-de-Provence and Les Baux, all within easy distance.

TOURIST OFFICES National: Maison de la France, 8 av. de l'Opéra, 75001 Paris Ⓣ 01/42 96 10 23 Ⓕ 42 86 08 94; Paris**:** 127 av. des Champs-Elysées Ⓣ 01/49 52 53 54; Avignon: 41 cours Jean Jaurès Ⓣ 04 90 82 65 11. UK: London Ⓣ 0891/244 123 (premium rate). US: New York Ⓣ 212/838 7800 Ⓦ http://www.maison-de-la-france.com:8000/

COUNTRY CODE Ⓣ 33

GERMANY

B erlin traditionally holds one of the country's largest New Year's Eve parties, with tens of thousands of people celebrating at the **Brandenburg Gate** to the sound of DJs and live bands. The year 2000 will also see a symbolic performance of the famous **Passion Play** in **Oberammergau**.

The biggest event taking place in Germany is **Expo 2000** in Hannover, with between twenty to forty million people expected to visit from June to October 2000.

Berlin

Almost every nightclub, bar and restaurant in **Berlin** hosts its own **Silvester** (New Year's Eve) party, with the best booked out months in advance. In 1999, Berlin will be competing with other world capitals to stage the biggest New Year's Eve party ever, with an hour-long fireworks display at the Brandenburg Gate; a series of 200 stages will be set up along the boulevard that runs through the Tiergarten to the gate, upon which thousands of performers will re-enact historical highlights of the last millennium. The event will be broadcast live, with the Chancellor delivering a speech to the nation from the Gate itself.

Berlin also traditionally stages a series of special New Year's performances at the **Komische Opera** (usually, Strauss's *Die Fledermaus*), the **Friedrichstadpalast** (revue with dancing, acrobats, and an orchestra), the **Varieté Wintergarten** (vaudeville), and the **Konzerthaus Berlin** (classical music). In addition, Berlin will be celebrating the renovation of the former Reichstag, which will become the new **Bundestag** (federal parliament) for reunified Germany when it opens in spring 1999.

The long-standing **Berliner Festspiele** (Berlin Festival), which features music, dance, theatre, film and literature, will be staging a special millennium festival, **2000: In Berlin**, which will run from May 14, 2000 to January 7, 2001.

Berlin Tourismus Marketing GmbH, Am Karlsbad 11, D-10785 Berlin
Ⓣ 030/2 64 74 80 Ⓕ 25 00 24 24; Berlin Festival GmbH, Budapester
Strasse 50, D-10787 Berlin Ⓣ 030/25 48 91 00 Ⓕ 25 48 92 30
Ⓦ http://www.berlinerfestspiele.de/ueberuns/aboutus.html (English)
Ⓦ http://www.berlinerfestspiele.de/berlinzweitausend/index.html (German)

Hannover

The first of its kind to take place in Germany, **Expo 2000** will be held at the refurbished **Hannover Exhibition Grounds** and the new development in the adjacent Kronsberg area. The exposition has already broken all records, attracting the support of the largest number of countries and international organisations at the highest level ever.

But even this show of solidarity has not guaranteed the smooth completion of Expo 2000. To begin with, the DM3 billion (£1b/US$1.7b) cost of construction should have been covered by sponsorship and ticket sales, but fears have now arisen that if fewer than twenty million visitors attend, Expo may face a loss. The government has already been forced to step in and underwrite DM500 million (£167m/US$282m) in loan guarantees.

There are also worries that the massive German pavilion will tower over all the other exhibits and generate complaints of 'national arrogance'. If it is successful, however, Expo will provide an international showcase for the new, reunified Germany on the brink of the twenty-first century. The exhibition runs from June 1 to October 31, 2000.

Expo 2000

Expo's theme, 'Mankind, Nature, Technology', explores and expands on Agenda 21 principles to emphasise sustainable development in the next millennium. It will feature numerous

Oberammergau

The Oberammergau Passion Play has its origins in an outbreak of the Black Plague in the seventeenth century, when the people of the village vowed to commemorate the life of Christ in a play every ten years if they were fortunate enough to survive. The first play took place in 1634, and has since grown from a simple peasant performance to a masterwork.

Passion Play 2000, which will take place between May 11 and September 24, 2000, is expected to be particularly dramatic during the symbolic year 2000, with 2000 villages taking part in over 100 performances.

Verkehrs-und Reisebüro Gemeinde, Oberammergau OHG, Mitgesellschafter abr-Reisebüro, Eugen-Pabst-Strasse 9a
Ⓣ 08822 1021 Ⓕ 08822 7325.

interactive and virtual technologies: one of the showpieces will be a multimedia, virtual reality cityscape which will be projected onto a site the size of thirteen football fields. Created by the French virtual reality wizard François Confino, the cost of this alone is approximately DM290 million (£100m/US$164m).

The main area comprises **The Universe of Visions**, a vast exhibition space where visitors are promised journeys into virtual worlds and the chance to propose their own solutions to global problems. Themed areas will explore topics such as how humans function, nutrition, health, information and communications, the future of work, mobility, energy, and technologies for the twenty-first century.

The designers are promising journeys through a virtual body, virtual tours of the cities of the world, subterranean voyages through energy systems, and many other interactive exhibits. A 2.5G 'elevator' will allow you to experience two and a half times the earth's gravitational pull, and a live link to the **MIR** space station will put you in touch with an educationalist who will be happy to answer visitors' questions. A shuttle will also take visitors to the **Emsland maglev track** (at 31km the longest in the world) for journeys at speeds in excess of 400km/hr on an experimental magnetic levitation train.

As well as the futuristic visions and sci-fi adventures in the Universe of Visions the exhibition will also contain around 160 national pavilions and an extensive **Arts and Culture Programme**. This will include at least one major event scheduled every evening during the 153-day event, encompassing opera, theatre, rock and pop concerts, computer animation and video art, dance and cabaret, painting and sculpture, magic and variety shows, fashion, film, and other entertainment.

Expo 2000 Hannover GmbH, D-30510 Hannover, Germany Ⓣ 0511/8404 136 Ⓕ 8404 180. Tickets go on sale on June 1, 1998 through appointed sales agents worldwide and offices of Deutsche Ban (German Railways) and the Expo Call Centre hotline Ⓣ 0/2000, operational from June 1, 1998.

Ⓦ http://www.expo2000.de/ or Ⓦ http://www.expo2000.de/index-e.html (contents in English)
Excellent site with more than 300 pages covering EXPO 2000, including detailed features concerning the central theme of sustainable development in the next century. Well designed and fast loading, the site also includes an award-winning EXPO for Kids section and live transmission of pictures from the exposition as it develops.

TRAVEL BRIEF

Major events taking place in Germany during the year 2000 will make it a hugely popular destination. It is advisable to book both transport and accommodation as early as possible.

GETTING THERE Over 100 international airlines, including the national carrier, Lufthansa, operate flights into Germany from across the globe, with the main international gateways at Frankfurt, Munich and Berlin. There will be additional direct flights to Hannover during Expo, with a new, large terminal at Hannover airport. There are excellent rail connections both within Germany and from surrounding countries. To cope with demand during Expo, there will be additional services to Hannover and a new railway station at Laatzen, next to the Expo site. Tickets for both Expo and Oberammergau will be on sale from mid-1998 at all Deutsche Bahn agencies worldwide.

ACCOMMODATION Within a two-hour radius of Expo there will be some 500,000 beds available. Within Hannover itself, however, the number drops to about 35,000 beds, 27,000 of them in private guest houses. Book early. Berlin will be crammed for New Year and the whole Oberammergau region full during the summer.

TOURIST OFFICES National: Deutsche Zentrale für Tourismus e.V. (DZT), Beethovenstrasse 69, D-60325 Frankfurt am Main Ⓣ 069/97 46 40
Ⓕ 75 19 03; Berlin: GmbH, Am Karlsbad 11, D-10785 Berlin
Ⓣ 030/2 64 74 80; Hannover: Ernst-August-Platz 2 Ⓣ 0511/30 140.
UK: London Ⓣ 0891/600 100 (premium rate; 24 hrs). US: New York
Ⓣ 212/661 7200; Los Angeles Ⓣ 310/575 9799
Ⓦ http://www.germany-tourism.de/

COUNTRY CODE Ⓣ 49

HOLLAND

Holland has no official millennium plans to date. Pubic parties are being planned in Den Helder's **Fort Kijkduin** and by the **Dutch Millennium Foundation** in Haarlem. The **Hague Appeal for Peace Conference** takes place in 1999.

Dutch Millennium Foundation

What do an illustrated poem, a poster on acid rain, a graphic showing zoo animals wandering through a deserted urban landscape, a countdown calendar and a desktop sculpture of the letter 'M' all have in common? The answer is that they are all artworks produced by the **Dutch Millennium Foundation** (Stichting Millennium), a group formed in 1987 by five friends whose aim is to 'explore the future together with musicians, artists, architects, and others'.

The foundation's five core members are supported by around 200 donors, who each year give an annual contribution amounting to the same number of Dutch guilders as the last two digits of the year (in 1998, for instance, it will be 98 guilders (around £30/US$49), but in the year 2000 it will be zero. Donations are used to fund a stylishly produced range of artworks, one for each year, which are then given as gifts on the annual donors' day. "We try to initiate ideas to help people think about time, and the future", says Pieter Buning, one of the founder members. "The word initiate is important – we want to try and do things which haven't been done before, and we provide people with the opportunity to express themselves on the future, and to share this amongst our donators and, quite often, a larger audience."

The donors' day always has a theme on some aspect of time and the millennium, as do most of the artworks they produce. The five founder members (Jaap Sluis, Johan de Kleuver, Pieter Buning, Jasper Nijk and Henk van der Leen) have even jetted off to New York in their search for millennial inspiration. "What keeps us going are the three 'Gs' of *Geloof*, *Gedrevenheid* and *Gekte*", says Henk van der Leen, "probably quite a mouthful of Dutch, but translated this means Belief, Motivation and Madness!"

The foundation has collaborated with the **Academy of Photography** in Haarlem, their home town, to run a millennium project each year for students, who have to provide a photographic vision of the millennium. The collection, so far comprising around ninety photos, will be on display in the year 2000. They have also planted a 'living sculpture' of trees in Haarlem city's woods, the **Haarlemmerhout**. The two rows of trees have been planted at angles and trained along steel cables to form a living arch, 'an *estafette* (a relay) through time'.

The foundation's most ambitious project to date, however, has been the grandly titled **Monument to the Twentieth Century** in downtown Haarlem. The twin arcs of the monument house two 'clocks', neon ribbons that light up as time passes – one on an annual cycle, the other on a daily cycle. A conventional clock and a digital countdown clock are also built into the monument. The project was inaugurated by the mayor on November 23, 1995 on the 750-year anniversary of the city's founding, and is likely to be one of the main focal points of Haarlem's New Year's Eve celebrations on December 31, 1999. The Foundation is currently looking for partners to help them create a twin of their millennium monument somewhere else in the world.

Stichting Millennium, PO Box 5467, 2000 GL Haarlem Ⓣ 023/5320217
Ⓕ 5320346 Ⓔ millenum@xs4all.nl Ⓦ http://www.xs4all.nl/~millenum/

The Living Planet Campaign

Launched at the start of the last 1000 days before the millennium, the World Wide Fund for Nature's Living Planet Campaign is designed to focus attention on key regions crucial to the conservation of global biodiversity. These regions, the Global 200, include areas already well known for their rich biodiversity, such as the Galapagos, the Amazon Basin, the savannas of East Africa, the Great Barrier Reef, temperate rainforests of the Pacific Northwest, and the rainforests of Borneo, New Guinea, and the Congo Basin.

It also highlights less familiar areas, such as the forests of New Caledonia, the coral reefs of the Sulu Sea, temperate forests in Appalachia and China, deserts in Mexico, Africa's Rift Valley lakes, and Mississippi's Piedmont rivers. WWF wants to motivate people 'to make the last part of the century a turning point in the conservation of the Global 200' by making Gifts to the Earth, which can range from funding anti-poaching controls to campaigning against roads or dams. Several governments have already pledged increased conservation measures under this scheme.

Local WWF offices, or The Living Planet Campaign, Boulevard 12, 3707 BM Zeist, Holland Ⓣ 30/69 37 346 Ⓕ 69 37 383
Ⓔ WWF2000@WWFNET.ORG Ⓦ http://www.panda.org/livingplanet/

Events

Den Helder

December 31, 1999

Den Helder's **Fort Kijkduin** will be the setting for a New Year's Eve spectacular. The fort, built during the Napoleonic era, has a 360° view of the sea, beach and sand dunes from its upper level, which has room for several bands, and a labyrinth of tunnels below, each of which will have its own bar and entertainment.

Stichting Entree-2000, Middelzand 2611 CK Den Helder, the Netherlands
Ⓣ 023/642305 Ⓔ entree@tref.nl Ⓦ http://www.tref.nl/kvnh/entree-2000

The Hague Appeal for Peace 1999:
Congress Centre, the Hague

May 11–16, 1999

In 1899 the first International Peace Conference was held in the Hague with the aim of developing mechanisms of international law to contribute to disarmament, the prevention of war, and the peaceful settlement of disputes. Followed by a second conference in 1907, it led to the establishment of the International Court of Justice and the Permanent Court of Arbitration (both based in the Hague), as well as several conventions that played in key role in the development of international humanitarian law. A Third Hague Peace Conference proposed for 1915 was ironically cancelled due to the outbreak of World War I.

The Hague Appeal for Peace 1999 Conference will bring together a wide variety of organisations, activists, citizens and world leaders to discuss new projects and initiatives for the promotion of peace in the twenty-first century, including disarmament, peace-keeping, international law, gender issues, human rights and sustainable development. The organisers are hoping for 5000–10,000 participants.

Hague Appeal for Peace, The Hague, c/o IALANA (International Association of Lawyers Against Nuclear Arms), Anna Paulownastraat 103, 2518 BC The Hague, Netherlands Ⓣ 070/3634484 Ⓕ 3455951 Ⓔ ialana@antenna.nl. US: Hague Appeal for Peace, New York, c/o WFN (World Federalist Movement), 777 UN Plaza, New York, NY 10017, US
Ⓣ 212/687 2623 Ⓕ 599 1332 Ⓔ hap99@igc.apc.org

COUNTRY CODE Ⓣ 31

ICELAND

I n the year 2000 Iceland will be commemorating the **Millennium Anniversary** of the first European voyage to North America, which was led by Icelandic-born Leifur Eriksson (Leif the Lucky). Reykjavik is one of the nine European Cities of Culture 2000, and the country will also be celebrating the anniversaries of various national cultural institutions such as the Icelandic Symphony Orchestra, the National Theatre of Iceland, and the National Broadcasting Service. The country will also be marking a **Millennium of Christianity**. In July 2000 there will also be an **International Viking Festival**, and in November 2000 a large-scale **Nordic Cultural Festival**, in conjunction with the meeting of the Nordic Council.

Reykjavik

The city's theme as one of the European Cities of Culture 2000 is 'Culture and Nature', and although no details are yet available Reykjavik will be highlighting children's and young people's culture and participating in several major joint projects, such as travelling exhibitions, in co-operation with the eight other cultural capitals. The **Reykjavik Arts Festival**, a biennial programme of international artists and performers, will be staging a special programme in the summer of 2000 between May and June.

Reykjavik 2000, Kirkjutorgi 4, 101 Reykjavik Ⓣ 575 2000 Ⓕ 575 2099
Ⓔ reykajavik2000@domino.europe.is

Millennial Meeting at Thingvellir

Thingvellir holds a special place in Iceland's history, as it was the original meeting place of the Icelandic Parliament over a thousand years ago. Protected as a National Park, this beautiful location in a natural amphitheatre is still used on important occasions by Parliament, although they have to obtain permission from a body known as the Thingvallanefnd, who control events there.

Since 1991 the Virginia-based Millennium Institute has been lobbying for a Millennium Summit of the world's spiritual leaders and heads of state to be held on the Thingvellir in the summer of 2000, to achieve what they describe as 'an enormously powerful, planetary event at the entry into the twenty-first century'. They envisage 'fifty to one hundred spiritual leaders assembled under a beautiful tent at one end of the upper flats of Thingvellir. In front of the spiritual leaders would be a stone table, and beyond the table on the plane would be an even larger colourful tent, and under this tent would be assembled the almost two hundred heads of state of the world'. Each of the leaders would then read out their nation's pledge of what it will do for the earth in the twenty-first century, and place their pledges on the stone table. At the end of the ceremony, the pages would be bound into the *Earth Book, 2000,* which would be translated into numerous languages as 'a palpable symbol of what the peoples of the Earth committed themselves to on the occasion of their entry into the third millennium'.

Why Thingvellir? Because Iceland is one of the few places in the world to which every head of state would be comfortable accepting an invitation. It has long summer nights (important if everybody's going to have time to read their scroll), and it is at the joining of the European (Eastern) and American (Western) tectonic plates, 'a place that holds the world together'.

The Icelandic Parliament is naturally fairly sceptical about the feasibility of staging this biblical scenario in their tiny country, and there is also the problem of accommodating the retinues of the 300 most important people in the world. But, says the Institute, guests would be strictly limited to 'the spiritual leaders and heads of state, their principal spouse or partner, a single aid or assitant, and no news media'. Imagine: no make-up artists, wardrobe assistants and hairdressers, press assistants and spin doctors, policy wonks and ministers, chefs and caterers, journalists, sound assistants, researchers and camera operatives...now that really is millennial thinking!

TRAVEL BRIEF

With only four or five hours of winter time daylight, this may not be the most obvious place to welcome in the New Year, but think of wallowing in a steaming outdoor hot spring, under clear winter stars, a drink in one hand and the prospect of a day's snow mobiling and suddenly it all becomes very appealing. The real rush comes in mid-summer (June–August), with festivities added by Reykjavik's role as a European City of Culture.

GETTING THERE Several international airlines operate flights into Reykjavik, but the largest of the carriers is Icelandair, with seven departure cities in the US and two in the UK. It is worth booking ahead during peak season.

ACCOMMODATION Reykjavik has a reasonably large supply of comfortable hotels, most three-star or above. Elsewhere in the country there is a much more limited supply of accommodation. Book ahead in peak season.

TOURIST OFFICES National: Laikjirgata 3, Reykjavik Ⓣ 552 7488 Ⓕ 562 4749; Reykjavik: Skolavordustig 2 Ⓣ 551 5862. UK: London Ⓣ 0171/388 7550. US: New York Ⓣ 212/885 9747/9700 Ⓦ www. rvk.is/

COUNTRY CODE Ⓣ 354

IRELAND

Throughout the whole of Ireland there will be huge celebrations for **St Patrick's Day 1999**, which has been earmarked as a major 'homecoming festival' to mark the millennium, an occasion for the entire Irish diaspora to come together from around the world and celebrate.

Projects taking shape throughout the country focus on Ireland's religious heritage, such as the walking routes along various medieval **Pilgrim Paths** being proposed by the Heritage Council. Those put forward so far include the Saint's Road on the Dingle Peninsula; St Kevin's Way in Glendalough; Balintubber Abbey to Croagh Patrick; Lough Derg; the Turas around Glencolmeille; St Declan's Way from Ardmore to Cashel; and Durrow to Clonmacnoise. It is hoped that the Pilgrim Paths will be finished by the summer of 2000. The Heritage Council is also planning a millennium project to identify and develop semi-natural woodlands around the country.

The Augustinian **Mayo Abbey** in the west of Ireland has been pooling local resources for the creation of the **Mayo Millennium Project**, an interpretative centre in a disused church on the site which will tell the story of the abbey's creation in the seventh century and its subsequent prominence in the region (it gave its name to County Mayo). The project will also involve links with Iona, Lindisfarne and the creation of the **Mayo Pilgrimage Trail**. The centre is due to open at Easter 2000.

Dublin

Dublin's **Millennium Clock** was one of the first to be put in place and one of the first to be removed, having survived only a few months. Since then, Dublin Corporation has identified a number of millennium projects which it hopes to find funding for, although many of these would have happened even without the millennium. They include a new **pedestrian bridge** over the River Liffey; **Project Tree 2000**, with plantings throughout the city; decorative lighting on the Liffey's bridges as part of a **Waters of Life** project; upgrading the landscaping and pedestrianising **O'Connell Street**, and an international **competition** to design the area in front of **Heuston** station.

NORTHERN IRELAND

Pyramids, domes, spires and arches are springing up elsewhere throughout the world, but Northern Ireland is
the only place that has the distinction of erecting a megalith,
or large standing stone (see box). In a thousand years' time it
may well be the only millennium project from the year 2000
to remain standing.

The biggest investment is the creation of the £100 million
Odyssey project in **Belfast**, which is one of the fourteen
Landmark Projects in the UK.

Elsewhere, **Downpatrick** is building the **St Patrick Visitor Centre**, which will portray the life and legend of the
saint, who was buried there. In **County Antrim** the historic
Gobbins Cliff Path, built during the Victorian era, is to be
restored at a cost of £4.5 million (US$7.4m).

Belfast: Odyssey Complex

Located in the Abercorn Basin in Belfast, the **Odyssey** complex will incorporate a world-class **Science Centre**, an
indoor arena, an IMAX theatre, and a range of shops and
leisure facilities. The Science Centre, under the direction of
the Ulster Museum, will feature five zones with interactive
displays focusing on 'Ourselves' (body, mind, health and
sports), 'Energy and Movement' (electricity, magnetism, air
and flight, water and boats), 'Communications', the 'Changing Earth', and an under eight's play area. The 300-seater
IMAX auditorium will feature an 18m by 20m screen. There
will also be exhibition areas, a 10,000-seater indoor sports
arena, and a central pavilion with fourteen-screen multiplex
cinema, shops and restaurants. Odysssey is scheduled to open
in 2000.

Odyssey Project, 35 Bedford Street, Belfast BT2 7EJ
Ⓣ 01232/278798 Ⓕ 278799.

The Strangford Stone

The plan to erect the Strangford Stone in County Down involves erecting a 25-tonne granite monolith on the shores of Strangford Lough in the Delamont County Park outside Killyleagh, creating a landmark for navigators and travellers around the lough. But the main idea behind the stone is to unite a thousand young people (who will help put it in place using only ropes and muscle power) in a common purpose, leaving the stone standing for generations to come as a symbol of their teamwork across divided communities. The stone, which is to be quarried from the nearby Mourne Mountains, will stand 10m high (1000cm – one for each year of the millennium) and will be the tallest megalith in Ireland or Britain. A simple rectangular shape, it will be unadorned, apart from a small panel showing the alignment of the planets on Midsummer's Day in June 1999, the day it is to be erected.

TRAVEL BRIEF

Ireland is more of a summer destination, but country cottages and other rural retreats are likely to be popular over New Year's Eve and Christmas 1999. With thousands of expat Irish descending on Dublin and other major cities for St Patrick's Day, there should be quite a celebration. In northern Ireland, it is more of a religious event for Catholics, with fewer street carnivals.

GETTING THERE There are numerous airlines operating flights into Dublin, with twelve from the UK alone. St Patrick's Day is always busy and 1999 (and possibly 2000 as well) will be far worse, particularly on transatlantic crossings. US passengers facing difficulties booking direct flights should fly to London and connect. Belfast is served by British Airways, British Midland, and Aer Lingus (connecting to the US via Dublin). Regular ferries shuttle between Wales, Scotland and Ireland; connecting services with the ferries are operated by Irish Railways (south) and Translink (north).

ACCOMMODATION The whole country will almost certainly be jam-packed over St Patrick's Day. Book as soon as possible to ensure your place of choice. Dublin Tourism operates a central credit-card reservation service

Ⓣ 01/605 7777. Accommodation in Belfast can be booked through the Tourist Information Centre Ⓣ 01223/246609.

TOURIST OFFICES (South) National: Baggot St Bridge, Dublin 2 Ⓣ 01/602 4000 or 602 4100; Dublin: Suffolk St, Dublin 2 Ⓣ 01/605 7700 Ⓕ 605 7749. UK: London Ⓣ 0171/493 3201. US: New York Ⓣ 212/418 0800 Ⓦ http://www.irelandtravel.ie (Ireland); US: Ⓦ http://www.irelandvacations.com./

(North) Northern Ireland Tourist Board, St Anne's Court, 59 North Street, Belfast BT1 1NB Ⓣ 01232/231221 Ⓕ 240960. UK: Ⓣ 0171/355 5040. US: Ⓣ 212/922 0101 Ⓦ http://www.ni-tourism.com

COUNTRY CODE (South) Ⓣ 353 (North) Ⓣ 44

ISRAEL AND PALESTINE

The ancient biblical sites of the **Holy Land** are likely to be the second busiest pilgrimage destination in the world (after Rome) in the year 2000. Between four to seven million visitors are expected, thanks, in part, to an unprecedented papal decree encouraging pilgrimages to **Israel** and the **Palestinian** territories. Pope John Paul II is planning a mass gathering of religious leaders in the Holy Land at the end of 1999. Spiritual leaders from Christian denominations, Islam and representatives of other religions such as the Dalai Lama will be invited to one of the largest meetings of religious leaders ever organised in an attempt to counter the hedonistic, secular parties taking place across the globe. Prayers will be read at the **Basilica of the Annunciation** in Nazareth and the **Holy Sepulchre** in Jerusalem, culminating in a service at the **Nativity Church** in Bethlehem.

Inevitably, the millennium has become highly politicised in a region where religious and geopolitical divisions run deep. What should have been a peaceful celebration of the anniversary of Christ's birth has become the focus of bitter recriminations over issues such as land rights, control of and access to holy sites, the allocation of millennium budgets and the battle for a share of the pilgrim dollar in the year 2000.

The site of the **Battle of Armageddon** as portrayed in Revelation is reportedly about to be transformed into a multimedia experience for tourists. The **Mount of Megiddo**, 45 miles north of Tel Aviv, is currently a partially excavated archaeological site, but the Israeli heritage authorities plan to create light shows and holograms to transport visitors back through 6000 years of Holy Land history. This 'virtual armageddon' will feature fourteen new multi-media visitor centres and sophisticated computer graphics, supplied by IBM, using a 'magic windows' system (said to be the next step beyond virtual reality) to bring the past alive. Work on the project, since dubbed 'Apocalypso', began in January 1998.

Meanwhile, a Californian couple are planning to stage a re-creation of the **Journey of the Magi**. Robin and Nancy Wainright plan to retrace the route travelled by the three wise men in search of the baby Jesus, starting out in the ancient town of Ur (Iraq) in August 1999 and travelling by camel and horse across 1500 miles of desert, mountains and steppe to reach Bethlehem on December 25, 1999. They are hoping that thousands will join them on their mission to spread peace and goodwill, and they also plan to initiate healthcare and water supply projects in villages they pass through, as well as raise US$2 million (£1.2m) in development aid.

[145]

Nazareth

Nazareth has been a key pilgrim centre for most of the past two millennia. Half of all tourists to Israel visit this celebrated Galilee town where the Annunciation took place and where Jesus spent most of his life. Nazareth has numerous historical sites relating to the Christian story, including the carpentry workshop of Joseph, the remains of Mary's home where Christian tradition says she received the message from the angel Gabriel that she was to give birth to the Son of God (two churches, one Greek Orthodox and one Roman Catholic, stand on this site), and the table where Jesus is said to have dined with his disciples.

In 1994 the Israeli government launched **Nazareth 2000**, an ambitious programme to rejuvenate the city in preparation for the influx of millennial pilgrims. Over US$100 million (£61m) is being spent on refurbishing historic houses in the **Old City**, connecting religious sites with scenic walkways, restoring the market, and resurfacing roads with ancient-style paving. Eight new hotels are also planned. "There is strong competition between Nazareth and the European holy cities over the year 2000 tourists, and Israel is racing time to assure its profit", said the director general of the Israeli Government Tourist Corporation. "We estimate our income from tourism in the coming decade to be a billion dollars."

Around 1.2 million pilgrims are expected to visit Nazareth in 2000, swamping its largely Arab population of around 60,000 (half Christians and half Muslims).

Bethlehem

In the West Bank town of **Bethlehem**, which was turned over to Palestinian control in 1995, the Palestinian president **Yasser Arafat** appointed his high-profile minister Dr Hanan

Ashrawi as commissioner of **Bethlehem 2000**. The organisation aims to bring together political and religious leaders (including the pope) for celebrations in Christ's birthplace at the millennium. The committee has drawn up an action plan in conjunction with UNESCO, covering cultural heritage, traffic and transportation, and economic and tourism development.

The ambitious cultural heritage project includes the renovation of important historic sites such as **Manger Square**, **Star Street** (the route taken by the patriarch at Christmas), the old **Bethlehem market**, historic centres in neighbouring **Beit Jala** and **Beit Sahour**, and the rehabilitation of historic homes to create community and cultural centres. The plan also includes the renovation of the historic **Solomon's Pools** and **Pools' Castle**. Most of these projects are unlikely to be finished in time for the millennium, however, given that around US$250 million (£153m) is needed to fund the action plan.

Celebrations in Bethlehem are likely to last for two years, from January 1, 1999 to December 31, 2000. There are plans to establish a Bethlehem's children's choir and proposals for an international-calibre opera. Invitations will also be extended to top artists, singers and theatre groups to stage performances during this period.

Bethlehem 2000, PO Box 2000, Bethlehem, Palestine ⓣ 02/742225 or 74226 ⓕ 742227 ⓔ bl2000@palnet.com.

Jerusalem

Established over 3000 years ago as the capital of Israel by King David, **Jerusalem's** long historical and biblical heritage has endowed it with a wealth of famous landmarks, shrines, antiquities and monuments. Considered a holy city by Jews, Christians and Muslims alike, Jerusalem's significance to the three monotheistic religions means that it is visited by thousands of pilgrims and tourists every day. The number of annual visitors is expected to swell to millions as the 2000-year anniversary of the birth of Jesus Christ approaches.

The city and surrounding areas contain a vast number of sites connected to Jesus's ministry in Jerusalem and his eventual crucifixion there. The **Temple Mount** was the site of the Jerusalem Temple, which played a key role in Jewish religious, political and economic life during the time of Jesus. Built by King Solomon in the tenth century BC, it was destroyed by the Babylonians in 587 BC and rebuilt in 516 BC. Judaic tradition holds that the **Ark of the Covenant** (containing fragments of Moses' tablets) rested in the 'Holy of Holies' inside the temple. The gospels report that Jesus came to Jerusalem to celebrate the feast of the Passover, and it was his teachings in the temple that eventually led the authorities to condemn him to death.

The temple was destroyed by Titus's Roman legions in 70 AD, and the site is now dominated by a Muslim shrine, the **Dome of the Rock**, which was built after the Muslim conquest of Palestine in the seventh century. The original **Western Wall**, which was left standing when the temple was destroyed, is visited by Jews from all over the world who face the wall when they pray.

One of Jerusalem's most sacred places of pilgrimage is the **Church of the Holy Sepulchre**, believed to have been the resting place of the body of Jesus after his crucifixion. His final path to **Calvary** from the **Garden of Gethsemani** is marked by the **Stations of the Cross**, locations that indicate incidents on the journey. The Christian tradition of devotion at the Stations of the Cross began with early Byzantine pilgrims, and by the eighteenth century the route had become known as the **Via Dolorosa**.

JERUSALEM TRAVEL BRIEF

With Jerusalem the world's holiest city and Bethlehem and Nazareth nearby, the authorities are expecting millions of pilgrims but no special arrangements are being made, so book well ahead.

GETTING THERE Most people visiting Israel arrive by air to Ben Gurion airport, between Tel Aviv (23km) and Jerusalem (4km). There are some internal flights, but distances are short and easily covered by road, with a superb bus system. El Al will put on extra flights to cater for the demand. There are ferries to Haifa from several cities in the eastern Mediterranean.

ACCOMMODATION There are no central hotel reservations in Israel, but several major international chains such as Holiday Inn, Hilton and Sheraton have a number of hotels in the country, for easy booking. Booking will be heavy, and luxury landmark hotels such as the famous King David are already filling up. Eight new hotels are under construction. Specialist pilgrim tours may have access to additional accommodation.

TOURIST OFFICES Tel Aviv: 5 Shalom 'Aleichem St Ⓣ 03/660 259 6061; Jerusalem: 24 King George St Ⓣ 02/675 4811 Ⓕ 625 3407; Municipal Information Office, 17 Jaffa Rd Ⓣ 02/625 8844. UK: London Ⓣ 0171/299 1111. US: New York Ⓣ 1-800/514 1188 (toll-free) or 212/499 5650; Chicago Ⓣ 1-800/782 4306; Dallas Ⓣ 1-800/472 6364; Los Angeles Ⓣ 213/658 7642 Ⓦ http://www.infotour.co.il/

PALESTINIAN TERRITORIES
TRAVEL BRIEF

Palestine is where it all started, 2000 years ago (or thereabouts). Bethlehem is a very different place these days, but with thousands of pilgrims flocking in, the local stables could well be back in use.
A useful contact is PACE (Palestinian Association for Cultural Exchange), PO Box 841 Ramallah, West Bank, Palestine Ⓣ / Ⓕ 02/998 6854 Ⓔ pace@planet.edu. Ⓦ http://www.planet.edu ~pace.

GETTING THERE There are no international airports in the Palestinian Territories. Fly into Tel Aviv and travel from there. Security varies from time to time, so always double-check before setting out and again at the checkpoints en route. Preferably, take an organised tour.

ACCOMMODATION It's estimated that Bethlehem will need around 5000 rooms to accommodate the flood of tourists expected. At present, accommodation is limited to just 840 rooms in seven hotels, with only another 250 rooms under construction. Many people will be obliged to stay in Jerusalem and go in on a day trip.

TOURIST OFFICES There are no Palestinian tourist offices. Information is usually available from Israeli offices. Palestinian tourism development is handled by the Ministry of Tourism in Bethlehem Ⓣ 02/741 581 Ⓕ 743 753.

COUNTRY CODE (Israel and Palestine) Ⓣ 972

ITALY

P lans are in full swing in Rome for the celebration of what Pope John Paul II has dubbed **The Great Jubilee** to mark the third millennium of Christianity. Estimates vary of how many pilgrims will descend on the holy city, with city authorities predicting between forty and sixty million and the Vatican (on the basis of previous jubilees in 1950 and 1975) expecting more like ten to fifteen million.

Bologna was the site of the first university in Europe a thousand years ago, and in 2000 it will be one of the nine European Cities of Culture.

In **Turin Cathedral** the **Holy Shroud**, the cloth that was wrapped round the body of the crucified Christ according to Catholic tradition, is to have a special showing for the millennium. The last time the shroud was put on display in September 1987, three million pilgrims made the journey to see it.

Rome

The Pope will usher in the new millennium by banging on the Holy Door of St Peter's Basilica with the traditional silver hammer. Elsewhere, visitors may find that jack-hammers rather than silver hammers will mark the holy pilgrimage: construction work for the jubilee is taking place on 86 building sites around the capital and, if the Holy Year in 1975 is anything to go by, much of it will still be going on as pilgrims start to arrive.

One of the most controversial construction projects was a proposed mile-long tunnel close to the Vatican near the Castel Sant'Angelo (a fortress built to house the tomb of Emperor Hadrian). Archaeologists uncovered ancient Roman buildings which may contain a number of important tombs around Hadrian's burial site, and the tunnel has now been abandoned. A proposed widening of the motorway from the airport into the city has already been reduced from four lanes to three; a new ring road, which was meant to have doubled in size, is now only to be enlarged on sections near the Vatican. A new underground linking the Colosseum and the Vatican has already been abandoned.

One project that still looks feasible is the restoration of the **Colosseum**, which is undergoing a facelift with improved public access paid for by the Banco di Roma. Additionally, the **Borghese Picture Gallery**, closed for the last twelve years due to stabilisation works on the building, reopened in 1997. The city also plans to reorganise access to areas that will be popular with pilgrims, including the **Basilica of St Peters, St Paul Outside the Walls, St John Lateran** and **San Lorenzo**. More bus stops, bus shelters and two new tram lines are to be provided.

The Vatican had planned to built 50 new churches to mark the Great Jubilee, although it now seems likely that only 25 will be built. One of the most prominent will be the **Church of the Year 2000**, which has been designed by the distinguished New York architect Richard Meier. The church, which bears some resemblance to a cut-down version of the Sydney Opera House, is based on 'a series of displaced squares and four circles'.

There are also unconfirmed plans for a spectacular, **Ben Hurstyle Chariot Race** which will run from the Imperial Forum in Rome, via the Colosseum, and end at the Circus Maximus; the chariot race is intended to mark the millennium on the anniversary of the city's foundation on April 21, 1999. Rome was turned down for the 2004 Olympics in favour of Athens, and so Italy's National Olympic Committee has decided to hold an unofficial Olympics, the **Holy Games of the Holy Year**, which will be a rally of around 15,000–20,000 athletes from five continents to be held 'under the gaze of the pope'.

Great Jubilee 2000, Vatican City, 00120 Europe Ⓣ 06/698 82828 Ⓕ 698 81961 Ⓦ http://www.roma2000.it/
Information about events and services in Rome in the run-up to the Jubilee. Italian and English.

Bologna

The city's theme as a cultural capital is 'Information and Communication'. As part of its programme for the year 2000 Bologna will be opening a number of new or refurbished museums and other cultural institutions, including a multimedia library, a library of the arts and theatre, a museum of Jewish culture, a musical heritage museum, and a centre focusing on architectural heritage. Events in the pipeline include art exhibitions, festivals, and musical and theatrical shows.

Bologna 2000, via Oberdan 24, 40126 Bologna Ⓣ 051/204606 Ⓕ 268636.

Roma2000 Card

ROME TRAVEL BRIEF

Work is falling behind on many of the major projects to improve Rome's roads, underground and tram lines. Expect the city to be chaotic over Christmas and the New Year.

GETTING THERE There are direct scheduled services into most major Italian cities from cities across Europe, including several major UK airports. Most longhaul flights, including those from the US, serve only Milan and Rome. There will be extra flights to cater for the increased traffic, but it is still advisable to book as early as possible. Italy has an excellent rail system with links to the European TGV network.

ACCOMMODATION Due to shortages in Rome, plans are in hand to open local convents and monasteries to pilgrims. Book as soon as possible.

TOURIST OFFICES National: ENIT, Via Marghera 2, 00185 Rome Ⓣ 06/49 711 Ⓕ 446 3379; Rome: Via Parigi 11 Ⓣ 06/488 991; Vatican Information Office, St Peter's Square Ⓣ 06/698 4466 or 698 4866. UK: London Ⓣ 0171/408 1254. US: New York Ⓣ 212/245 4822; Chicago Ⓣ 312/644 0996; Los Angeles Ⓣ 310/820 1898 or 820 1959 Ⓦ http://www.ipzs.it/enit/enitel.html

COUNTRY CODE Ⓣ 39

NEW ZEALAND

The row between Pacific nations over sunrise times on
January 1, 2000 (see FAQs) has also affected New
Zealand, leading to a bitter battle between towns on the
North Island's east coast who are squabbling over a time dif-
ference for sunrise measured in seconds.

The town of **Gisborne**, on the North Island's northeast
tip, has for many years promoted itself as the first place to
greet each new day and holds an annual **First Light Festival** between Christmas and New Year's Day which attracts
up to 40,000 visitors. Organisers of this event hope to pull in
at least 70,000 people for the millennium celebrations, and
have been lobbying the government to declare Gisborne 'the
first official city in New Zealand to see the light of the new
millennium'.

But in May 1997 the government survey department, Ter-
ralink, released figures showing that **Te Mata Peak**, just outside of the town of **Hastings** further down the coast, would
see the sunrise before Gisborne's **Kaiti Hill**. Hastings was
immediately galvanised into action and set about promoting
'Hastings – the Millennium 2000 City', much to the dismay
of Gisborne. "We didn't want to take away any of their lime-
light", says Megan Williams, chair of Hastings' Millennium
Committee, "we prefer to stick to the facts...Te Mata Peak
will see the sunrise first." But in Gisborne they're not taking
this news lying down, and have switched the focus instead to
Mount Hikurangi, which is 1354m higher than Te Mata,
although it is more than fifty miles north of the city. "The
peak outside Hastings is not higher than Mount Hikurangi,

which is in the Gisborne district", says Caroline Taylor of **Events Gisborne**. "Hikurangi is the first land mass in New Zealand to see the new day, Gisborne the first city – end of story!"

Although Hastings is promoting 'an uninterrupted, high, clear view of the millennium sunrise from Te Mata Peak a few minutes ahead of anyone else in the world', the fact is that this whole dispute centres on mere seconds.

In 1997 New Zealand set up a **Millennium Board** to co-ordinate activities and 'ensure that the celebrations reflected the unique values, heritage, indigenous culture and identity of New Zealanders'. With a budget of NZ$10–25 million (£3.5–9m/US$6–14m), the board is considering a number of proposals including a **Millennium Bell** ('the largest tuned bell in the world'), a world children's festival, an international futures conference, an ECO house, and a variety of exhibitions. One of the most unusual ideas, which may well be copied elsewhere in the world, is the **Time Vault** project.

New Zealand Millennium Office, PO Box 805, Wellington
℡ 04/495 7266 ℻ 494 0684.

The Millennium Time Vault

"Our vision is to provide you with a vehicle to send your message to your children's children, to seal the voices and images of you and your family in a time capsule and send it into the future", says sculptor Denis Hall, the creator of the Millennium Time Vault.

Costing around NZ$3 million (£1m/US$1.8m), the huge underground chamber, topped off by a 15m-high pyramid, will be built during the year 2000 and sealed up on the first day of 2001. Potential earthquake-free sites are still being investigated, but one of the prime contenders is the 2000ft-high Belmont Hill close to Wellington, where the pyramid will rise up amidst a panorama of the city, the ocean and the mountains.

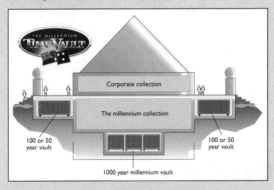

The main vault will contain the Millennium Collection, a treasure-trove of everyday objects, art works, keepsakes, icons, pictures, documents, videos, letters, artifacts, or simply messages to the people of the fourth millennium. There are also plans to store DNA samples of endangered species. Equipment such as computers and video and CD-rom players will be sealed away safely so that the inheritors of the vault will have access to archive material stored on formats which, by then, will no doubt appear antiquated.

Designed to be maintenance-free, the vault will be sealed with a huge concrete slab, bearing the message that it must remain undisturbed until the year 3000. "Any thief who wanted to gain entry would need heavy machinery or explosives to break in", says its designer. But he has not ruled out the possiblity that people in several hundred years' time might be tempted to take a peek inside to check the contents. "It's possible that before 1000 years are past, the museum curators will convince the authorities that the need to have the contents protected by twenty-fifth century technology will be greater than the need to honour our intentions", he added.

The 1000-year capsules will be suitcase-sized, high-impact carry cases (of the type used for video cameras) and will cost around NZ$2000 (£700/US$1200). Fifty- and one-hundred-year capsules will also be available, but these less expensive varieties, costing around NZ$180 (£65/US$105), will be buried in separate containers around the main pyramid so as not to disturb it when they are unearthed in 2050 and 2100.

Time Vault 2000, PO Box 27378, Wellington, New Zealand
Ⓣ 04/855 8290 Ⓕ 385 7470 Ⓔ office@timevault-2000.co.nz
Ⓦ http://www.timevault-2000.co.nz/
Contains a reservation form for a time capsule.

Events

Auckland: America's Cup 2000

The world's most prestigious yacht race, the **America's Cup 2000** takes place in the sailing waters around Auckland harbour from February 26 to March 26, 2000. Despite some teams (including one from Australia) withdrawing because of the high cost of port facilities in Auckland, a record number of eighteen challengers have entered for the race, including teams from Britain, France, Hong Kong, Italy, Japan, Russia, Spain, Switzerland, and the US.

Canterbury: Turning Point 2000

Established in 1995 by Christchurch City Council, **Turning Point 2000** aims to involve communities right across the province of Canterbury in a series of events and projects throughout the year 2000 up until New Year's Eve. It is one of the few organisations to have already timetabled a special event to greet the dawn on January 1, 2001, the 'official' start of the next millennium. The celebrations begin with a 24-hour New Year's Eve party in **Christchurch's Hagley Park** (around 200,000 are expected), linked by telecast to other events nationally and internationally. This will be followed by **Karanga at Dawn**, a Maori ceremony to greet the new day, at Godley Heads and a Sunrise Breakfast at Brighton Beach. In January/February there will be a **Science and Technology Exhibition** and annual events, such as the **Summertime Festival, Heritage Week** and **Art Festivals**, will be developed around Turning Point 2000's theme of 'Looking Back, Looking Forward'. Other projects include **Highway 2000** (landscaping the coastal state highway), **Gardens 2000**, **Port Hills 2000** (regenerating native forest and other developments), **TuTangata 2000** (building a *waka*, or Maori war canoe), and publishing various histories of the region.

Turning Point 2000, 392 Moorhouse Avenue, PO Box 237, Christchurch
Ⓣ 03/379 2008 Ⓕ 379 7131.

Gisborne: eco2000

Eco2000 aims to promote sustainable land management to an international audience as part of the Gisborne celebrations.

Events planned throughout 2000 include field days, seminars, and demonstrations on Maori land use, viticulture, farming, forestry, and urban sustainability.

Eco2000, PO Box 404, Gisborne Ⓣ 06/862 8435 Ⓕ 862 8835
Ⓔ eco2000@gisborne.org.nz Ⓦ http://www.gisborne2000.org.nz/eco.html

First Light Festival

Events Gisborne is co-ordinating a wide range of activities including the **First Light Festival**, an umbrella festival covering numerous events (including windsurfing championships, beach volleyball and the Gisborne Stampede). As part of the festival there will be a **New Year's Eve Party** in the town centre, with live entertainment around the Town Clock and Millennium Clock. The **First Light Te Kowhai Music Festival** will take place at Muriwai, with a spectacular view of Poverty Bay and the first sunrise, featuring Maori culture and bands from New Zealand and overseas. There are also plans for **Sea-Going Canoes** from seven Pacific nations to converge on Gisborne, 'coming through the sunrise on the first day of the new millennium'.

The **First Light Mardi Gras** will take place on January 1, 2000; this annual, family-oriented event features various entertainment and local arts and crafts. The city will also be hosting the **New Zealand Hot Rod Nationals** (December 29, 1999–January 2, 2000), with over 2000 participants, and welcoming 2000 cyclists on the **First to the Sun** ride, which starts in Auckland and takes in the Coromandel and East Cape before arriving in Gisborne.

Events Gisborne, PO Box 747, Gisborne Ⓣ 06/868 1568 Ⓕ 868 1368
Ⓔ info@firstlight.co.nz Ⓦ http://www.gisborne2000.og.nz/
Well-organised site with details on the First Light Festival and other events.

Ngati Porou Celebrations 2000

Te Runanga O Ngati Porou have organised a festival that includes cultural, recreational and sporting events as well as four-wheel drive trips and sunrise treks to Mount Hikurangi for a dawn ceremony.

Te Runanga O Ngati Porou, PO Box 226, Ruatoria
ⓣ 06/864 8121 Ⓕ 864 8806.

Odyssey's End 2000

An exclusive, 24-hour party in Gisborne is being planned by **Club Odyssey's End**, which has contracted to lease a fifty-acre site on the city's waterfront overlooking Poverty Bay's horizon, where the sun will rise. The main events will take place in a newly constructed stadium and will feature performances by a thousand Maori warriors as well as international entertainment acts, dramatic sunset and midnight ceremonies, a dawn ceremony, and a huge fireworks and laser show. Odyssey's End is hoping to attract up to 20,000 for the event.

Odyssey's End 2000, Future Pacific Publishing, PO Box 56 595 Dominion Road, Auckland ⓣ 09/623 1560 Ⓕ 623 0639 Ⓔ odyssey@futurepac.co.nz Ⓦ http://www.futurepacific.co.nz
Includes more details on events and a membership form. Because of the difficulties of accommodating so many people in Gisborne, Odyssey's End is planning to bring ticket-holders into and then out of Gisborne over a 32-hour period by road, rail, air and sea.

Servant 2000

Around 20,000 Christians from around the world are expected to participate in this ten-day, family-oriented rally, which will include a sunrise service on the beach and a millennial service and evening concert on January 1, 2000.

Servant 2000, Ray Sheldrake, 87 Ormond Road, Gisborne ⓣ 06/868 8053 Ⓦ http://www.gisborne2000.org.nz/serv.html

Te Runanga O Turanganui A Kiwa

Te Runanga O Turanganui a Kiwa is planning city-wide celebrations that will include a **Voyaging Canoes Pageant** involving wakahourua (double-hulled canoes), wakataua (war canoes) and waka-ama (racing canoes), all converging on Turanganui a Kiwa at the same time. The canoe pageant will form part of a **Multicultural Festival**. There are also plans for a **Cultural Centre**, the focus of which will be an enormous carving, **Whakairo Nunui**, which will be the biggest of its kind in the world.

Te Runanga O Turanganui A Kiwa, Barry Tupara
Ⓣ 06/867 8109 Ⓕ 867 8208.

Hamilton: Millennium Marathon

'The first marathon in the world of the new millennium' is to take place in the city of Hamilton, starting just after dawn (6am) and winding its way around the city on a 'relatively flat course'. A 10km fun run and a 5km walk will take place alongside the marathon. The main event is expected to attract around 4000 entrants.

The Millennium Marathon, PO Box 10-106, Te Rapa, Hamilton
Ⓣ 07/849 1782 Ⓕ 849 1789 Ⓔ info@hamilton.events.co.nz
Ⓦ http://www.marathontour.com/nz.htm

Hastings: Te Mata Peak

Hastings is planning a number of events, including a huge wine festival. One of the main focal points, however, is likely to be **Te Mata Peak**, which rises up to the south of the town. A large part of the peak is privately owned, and one landowner who has already built an amphitheatre in the side of the hill is expected to host a party for up to 1000 people. The top of the peak is a popular hang-gliding and para-gliding launch spot, and no doubt many flyers will want to fling themselves off at dawn. But the Trust

The Antarctic Sweepstakes

Who will be the first person to 'enter' the next millennium? Greg Wright suggests that "no one could be closer to the action than someone who is splayed out over the South Pole itself within the Amundsen-Scott station's geodesic dome...perhaps stretching a bit in the direction of longitude 180°." His proposal for the World Millennium South Pole Sweepstakes is for an international body such as the UN to declare this spot 'ground zero', and for it to organise a global competition for people willing to travel to the South Pole so that they could be officially declared the first person in the world to see the new millennium. 'The purpose of this exercise besides one more media angle on an already media-drenched millennium, is to raise money to serve one or more of the many vital needs and tasks for the next millennium', says Wright. He suggests a UN-administered Millennuim Biosphere Fund or even a World Mini-Loan Fund to finance micro-enterprises in the developing world.

World Millennium South Pole Sweepstakes, 14161 Riverside Drive #3, Sherman Oaks, CA 91423. Ⓣ (818) 784 0325; Ⓕ (818) 981 6835 Ⓔ greg@newciv.org

which owns this land has not yet decided whether the public will have access. "The logistics of this are quite daunting if everybody wanted to be there", says Megan Williams of the Hastings Millennium Committee. "However, I can assure you that there will be lots going on and the ridge line is quite extensive."

Hastings Millennium Committee, 404 Alexandra Street, Hastings, Hawke's Bay Ⓣ 06/878 0500 Ⓕ 878 5627 Ⓦ http://www.hawkesbay.com/millenn.html

Pacific Tall Ships Festival 2000

A replica of Captain Cook's ship *The Endeavour* will lead a large fleet of tall ships into the waters where Cook sailed

when he became the first European to chart New Zealand's coastline in 1769. Most of the recognised ships in Australasia, as well as others from the US, Spain, Germany and the Czech Republic, have already entered for the festival.

The fleet sets out from Wellington on December 10, 1999, arriving in Gisborne on December 28. Some of the ships will set sail for the International Date Line, less than 100 miles due east from Gisborne, to greet the new millennium. After the New Year they will leave for Tauranga, Auckland and the Bay of Islands. The itinerary will coincide with the **America's Cup 2000** to be held in Auckland in late January.

NZ Organising Committee, Pacific Tall Ships Festival 2000, PO Box 747, Gisborne, New Zealand
Ⓣ 06/867 2049 Ⓕ 867 9265 Ⓔ info@tallships2000.org
Ⓦ http://www.enternet.co.nz/client/personal/steve/
Contains an entry list, the itinerary, and registration forms.

Boy's 'Time Bomb' Solution

A 14-year-old Christchurch, New Zealand boy, Nicholas Johnson, gained worldwide media coverage in September 1997 with claims that he had written a programme that would help defuse the 'millennium time bomb'. Johnson's Beyond 1999 programme is designed to detect whether a computer can handle the date switch and make the necessary adjustments if it cannot. After the programme was revealed in a Christchurch business magazine the story was picked up by CNN, followed by the world's press. The boy's fame may be short-lived – there are already numerous programmes on the market that claim to deal with the problem – but at least he won't be unemployed when he leaves school. He has already had a firm offer of work from the international computer company Digital.

TRAVEL BRIEF

New Zealand is always a popular Christmas and New Year destination. The North Island will be hosting numerous events on New Year's Eve 1999 and combined with the Tall Ships Race and the America's Cup fleet visiting in January, the country is going to be heaving. The Olympics in Australia will bring another tidal wave of visitors in Sept/Oct.

GETTING THERE There are regular direct services to Auckland from the UK, US, Australia and other world centres, with several large airlines, including the national carrier, Air New Zealand, who also operate domestic schedules.

ACCOMMODATION Book now, although it may already be too late. The good thing is that New Year is in high summer in the southern hemisphere, so you could always camp outdoors.

TOURIST OFFICES National: Level 11, AA Centre, 99 Albert St (PO Box 6727 Wellesley St Mail Centre) Auckland ⓣ 09/379 7948; Auckland: 1st Floor, Lufthansa House, 36 Kitchener St, Auckland ⓣ 09/358 3644 ⓕ 377 2154. UK: London ⓣ 0839/300 900 (premium rate). US: New York ⓣ 212/832 8482; Los Angeles ⓣ 310/395 7480. Australia: Sydney ⓣ 02/247 5222 ⓦ http://www.nztb.govt.nz/

COUNTRY CODE ⓣ 64

NORWAY

T he Norwegian **Millennium Commission** has set up a working group to try and establish ways to use the millennium to 'make Norway better situated to deal with changing processes in time by being engaged in what we can learn from other nations'. The Commission, with a budget of around two billion kroner (£200m/US$2.75m), is seeking ideas for celebrations that reveal 'signs of innovation, optimism, fellow feeling, responsibility and openness'. Few projects have yet been decided upon, but one that has been given the go-ahead, **Millennium Places**, demonstrates that the Norwegians are the only people in the world to have considered the plight of those with nowhere to go on New Year's Eve 1999. The project involves setting up 435 meeting rooms, one for each council, where anybody who wishes to can come to celebrate the millennium rather than remain alone. The hour before midnight will be filled with celebrations, and at two minutes to midnight everybody will light a candle 'in silence and thoughtfulness'. Every town and village will have fireworks displays, but the biggest will be in **Oslo**, where 75 million kroner (£6m/US$10m) has been allocated for pyrotechnic displays. Oslo is also celebrating its 1000-year jubilee.

Millennium Commission, Department of Culture, Norwegian Government, Oslo, Norway Ⓣ 22 54 12 50 Ⓕ 22 54 12 01 Ⓔ ggs@isaf.no

Bergen

The city of **Bergen** is one of the nine European Cities of Culture 2000. The city's theme will be 'Art, Work and

Leisure'. The programme is still under development but will focus on three main themes: Dreams (spring), Motions (summer) and Rooms (autumn). The first part, 'Dreams', will coincide with the **Bergen International Festival** in May. 'Motions' will involve regional events around the city, whilst 'Rooms' will focus on spaces within the city – meeting places, squares and public venues – and feature concerts, theatre and other events.

Kulturby Bergen 2000, DnB Frescohallen, Vagsalmenning 1, 5014 Bergen, Norway Ⓣ 55 55 2000 Ⓕ 55 55 2001.

Debt-free Millennium

As the millennium approaches, the total debt owed by developing countries now stands at a record US$2.2 trillion (£1.3tr). Africa alone spends four times as much on servicing debt as on health care and has to pay back £3 (US$5) in debt repayments for every £1 (US$1.50) donated as aid. A coalition called Jubilee 2000 wants the millennium to be celebrated with a one-off cancellation of the backlog of unpayable debt owed by the world's poorest countries.

Launched in 1996, Jubilee 2000 has been gathering momentum with remarkable speed, and in 1997 Jubilee 2000 movements were launched in Norway, Sweden, Germany, Austria, New Zealand, Australia, Ghana, Tanzania, Canada and the US. A petition which they hope will be the world's largest ever (the previous record is thirteen million signatures) is to be presented at the G7 Summit in 1999.

For a resource pack, the *Debt Cutters Handbook*, contact Jubilee 2000, PO Box 100, London SE1 7RT Ⓣ 0171/401 9999 Ⓕ 401 3999 Ⓔ j2000@gn.apc.org Ⓦ http://www.oneworld.org/jubilee2000

TRAVEL BRIEF

Icy fjords, floodlit cross-country skiing, brightly painted wooden houses and throat-grabbing aquavit are amongst the possibilities for New Year in Norway.

The downside is that it stays dark nearly all day – but during the summer the midnight sun will shine down on the festivities in Bergen, celebrating its year as a European City of Culture 2000.

GETTING THERE Flights are always busy over Christmas and New Year and during the peak summer holiday season (June–Aug); 1999 and 2000 are unlikely to be any different. Several airlines fly out of the UK to Oslo and Bergen; SAS are the main carriers from the US, with many of their flights connecting via Copenhagen. There are direct ferries from the UK (Newcastle–Bergen) on Color Line; alternatively, Scandinavian Seaways operate ferries from Harwich and Newcastle via Gothenburg.

ACCOMMODATION No problems anticipated.

TOURIST OFFICES National: PO Box 2893, Solli, Drammensvein 40, Oslo 0230 Ⓣ 22 03 44 00 Ⓕ 22 56 05 05; Oslo: Vestbaneplassen 1 Ⓣ 22 83 00 50 Ⓕ 22 83 81 50; Bergen: Bryggen 7 Ⓣ 55 32 14 80. UK: London Ⓣ 0171/839 6255. US: New York Ⓣ 212/885 970 Ⓦ http://www.tourist.no

COUNTRY CODE Ⓣ 47

PACIFIC ISLANDS

T he South Pacific islands will be one of the principal beneficiaries of the millennium celebrations, with thousands of people likely to book up 'once in a lifetime' trips to locations claiming to offer the first glimpses of the new dawn. Countries such as **Kiribati** (pronounced 'Kiribas') and **Tonga**, previously minnows in the South Pacific tourism lagoon, are gearing up for an unprecedented influx of tourists. The Pacific islands have, however, been at the very centre of the debate as to exactly where the sun will rise first on January 1, 2000.

Until recently, the Kingdom of Tonga could lay claim to being the first landfall west of the dateline, and therefore the first to witness the dawn of each new day. It promotes itself as 'the place where time begins' and even has an International Dateline Hotel in the capital Nuku'alofa. But when Kiribati 'moved' the International Date Line in January 1995, the Tongans were deprived of their title. Apparently furious at being out-manoeuvred by Kiribati, they appealed to the United Nations and also toyed with the idea of introducing daylight savings time so they could pip everyone else to the post.

The Tongans have had to put a brave face on it and are still going ahead with their millennium plans, which include building at least a dozen new hotels, resorts, and ecotourism lodges. "In my opinion, Kiribati moving the dateline does not affect us that much", says Tonga's director of tourism Semisi P. Taumoepeau. "We will be put back in the list of 'the first to see the New Year', of course, but we will maintain the claim that we are one of the first to see the new millennium as well as being the first kingdom to do so", he says. "It's unlikely that the International Dateline Hotel will change its name, and as far as I am aware there have been no lost bookings", he adds.

The Pacific nations have also cast aside their differences in order to promote the region as a whole and have set up the **South Pacific Millennium Consortium**, an offshoot of the Tourism Council of the South Pacific based in Fiji.

MILLENNIUM OF THE SOUTH SEAS
crossing the threshold of time

"Whilst we are doing our best to promote [the first sunrise], we are not stressing the point so that it becomes competitive", says Millennium Co-ordinator Mrs Bernadette Rounds Ganilau. "We are the Pacific and the dawn rises on all of us. It just so happens that one or two of us will receive the rays first. We are doing a solidarity thing so the whole of the South Pacific benefits and not just one or two countries."

The region will also benefit from the fact that you can experience the dawn there twice: first in those countries to the west of the dateline (such as Tonga, Kiribati and Fiji), and then again in those to the east (such as Samoa, the Cook Islands, Tahiti and Niue). The last place on earth to see the sunset on the old millennium is the westernmost tip of Savai'i Island in Samoa, just twenty miles from the dateline.

New Caledonia, American Samoa, Vanuatu, Tuvalu, Niue, Papua New Guinea and the Solomon Islands have not announced any plans so far for the millennium.

South Pacific Millennium Consortium, 3rd floor, FNPF Plaza, 343-359 Victoria Parade, PO Box 13119, Suva, Fiji ⓣ 304177 ⓕ 301995 ⓔ spice@is.com.fj ⓦ http://www.tcsp.com/millennium/mill.htm

Cook Islands

The Cook Islands to the west of the dateline are expecting large numbers of party-goers to arrive on December 31, 1999 for the start of a double celebration. A substantial group will arrive from Fiji, which is two hours' flying time away on the other side of the dateline. Islanders celebrate New Year's Eve with exuberant displays of drumming, singing and Polynesia's sensual traditional dancing. These dance shows, known as **kariori**, also involve traditional singing and plays and are usually followed by a traditional feast, the **umukai**, consisting of dishes baked in an underground oven.

TRAVEL BRIEF

GETTING THERE Air New Zealand flies from Australia, New Zealand, Hawaii, Tahiti and Fiji, with links to North America and Europe. Polynesian Airlines provides services from Australia and New Zealand via Samoa, with connections to Fiji and Tonga.

ACCOMMODATION Around half of the Cook Island's hotels are already fully booked, although you may be able to find rooms through tour operators. Backpackers' hostels and guest houses have space available, but book well in advance. Note that it is not permitted to land in the Cooks without a reservation, and sleeping on the beach is not permitted.

TOURIST OFFICE Tourism Cook Islands, PO Box 14, Rarotonga, Cook Islands Ⓣ 29435 Ⓕ 21435 Ⓔ tourisme@cookisland.gov.ck Australia: Sydney Ⓣ 02/9955 0446. New Zealand: Auckland Ⓣ 09/379 4140. UK: London, Tourism Council of the South Pacific Ⓣ 0181/392 1838. US: Los Angeles Ⓣ 310/641 5621; toll-free: 888/994 COOKS.

COUNTRY CODE Ⓣ 682

Fiji

Fiji is to the west of the dateline and misses out on the first dawn, but they're still planning to celebrate on the basis that the 180° meridian runs through the islands.

One of the biggest events will be **Millennium 2000 – Fiji Islands Festival**. This two-week global festival of music and arts is being produced by the California-based **Foundation of the Arts for Cultures and the Environment** (FACE). The Millennium 2000 festival will include a dusk-to-dawn New Year's Eve concert which may also involve **WOMAD** (The World of Music, Arts and Dance), a highly successful and well-established international festival. Festival events will include music and dance, arts and crafts, an interactive technology exposition, and an ecological exhibition. The festival, to be held on Momi Bay, near Nadi, will also feature a **Technology Pavilion** with Internet access for visitors wishing to send greetings home.

A major part of the festival will be a gathering of the indigenous tribal peoples of the world. Fijian high chiefs are planning to send delegations to perform traditional ceremonies of invitation to their counterparts in other countries, and the arrival ceremonies for these visiting dignitaries will mark the opening for the **Millennium 2000** festival.

There are also plans to stage a one-week, interdenominational **World Festival of Praise** in Suva, with a grand finale on January 2, 2000, when participants from around the world will give cultural performances from their home country. The **Ministry of Sound**, one of London's most successful nightclubs, is also planning a **New Year's Rave** in Fiji through its touring arm.

On its extreme northeastern tip at Udu Point there are plans to build a **Meridian Wall**. At a site high up on the hill, the 1km-long wall will be built with hollow bricks into which people can place stainless steel tubes which will be sealed as time capsules with messages for the future.

In addition to fireworks on New Year's Eve 1999, Fijians are also organising a **Fire Ceremony** that it is hoped will light the hilltops on dozens of inhabited islands. They are also planning to build a **Voyaging Canoe** which will be launched at dawn at the place where the dateline meets the sea. A **Time Capsule**, including photos, messages to the future and other items from festival participants, will be dedicated at the site and sealed for a thousand years.

National Millennium Committee, Fiji Visitors Bureau, GPO Box 92, Suva, Fiji
Ⓕ 300 970 Ⓔ marketing@fijifvb.gov.fj

FACE 6118 Glen Holly, Los Angeles, CA 90068, US
Ⓕ 461 5960 Ⓔ facefest@ix.netcom.com Ⓦ http://www.fiji2000.org

TRAVEL BRIEF

GETTING THERE Fiji is served by Air Pacific, Air New Zealand, Qantas, Korean and Royal Tongan Airlines, with 85 international flights per week.

ACCOMMODATION A wide range of accommodation is available in Fiji, from luxury resorts to backpackers' beach hostels. Some of the top hotels are already booked.

TOURIST OFFICES Fiji Visitors Bureau, Thomson Street, Suva, Fiji
Ⓣ 302/433 Ⓕ 300/970 Ⓔ infodesk@fijifvb.gov.fj Ⓦ http://www.fijifvb.gov.fj
Australia: Sydney Ⓣ 02/ 264 3399. New Zealand: Auckland Ⓣ 09/373 2133.
US: Los Angeles Ⓣ 310/568 1616.

COUNTRY CODE Ⓣ 679

Kiribati

Kiribati is well placed to take advantage of the millennium celebrations on New Year's Eve 1999 in view of the fact that, since it moved the dateline, three of its islands in the Line and Phoenix group witness the sunrise before anywhere else in the world. These are **Millennium Island** (05:43 local time), **Flint Island** (05:47), and **Kiritimati** (05:31).

Millennium Island has no infrastructure at all, and very little fresh water. There are no plans to build any facilities, and the president of Kiribati believes that if anything happens here, it will be on a do-it-yourself basis – in other words, there may be a flotilla of yachts converging from Pacific ports or even a cruise ship or two, but once they get there it's up to them to create an occasion.

On Kiritimati, by contrast, the islanders have big plans. (Kiritimati is the local translation of Christmas Island, so named by Captain Cook because he arrived there on Christmas Eve in 1777.) The millennium has been embraced with almost messianistic fervour by the islanders, who are fervently hoping for a gathering of world leaders who will proclaim the dawning of a new era as the sun rises over the Pacific horizon.

No plans have yet been finalised for the celebrations, but the islanders are holding a song-writing competition (such competitions are a central part of their culture), with the winning song being performed at the dawn ceremony.

Kiritimati has two enormous runways, built when the Americans and British carried out nuclear tests here in the 1950s and 1960s. These runways will be the landing site for the Japanese space shuttle in 2005, and since they're long enough to handle a space shuttle they can, of course, easily accommodate all other aircraft.

TRAVEL BRIEF

GETTING THERE Air Marshall connects Kiribati with international routes, and Air Nauru flies to/from Nauru. Aloha Airlines also has services between Hawaii and Christmas Island.

ACCOMMODATION The country has fewer than 100 hotel rooms and only four hotels of a reasonable standard (two in South Tarawa, one on Abemama, and one on Kiritimati). Nasda, the Japanese space agency, is

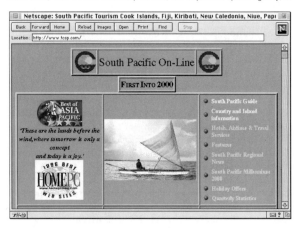

building a 150-room hotel on Kiritimati to accommodate crew and technicians from the shuttle programme. The official view is that anyone who wants to stay in a hotel is going to have to pay premium prices for the privilege. However, the president has said that independent travellers will not be ripped off and he is happy to extend a traditional welcome to anyone who wants to come provided they are prepared to stay in the *maneabas* (large, palm-thatched meeting houses) or local guest houses.

TOURIST OFFICES Kiribati Visitors Bureau, PO Box 261, Bikenibeu, Tarawa, Republic of Kiribati Ⓣ 26157 Ⓕ 26233. There are no national Tourist Offices overseas.

COUNTRY CODE Ⓣ 686

Samoa

Samoa is the furthest landmass to the east of the International Date Line and, as such, will be the last to witness the end of the twentieth century. Samoa (formerly Western Samoa) consists of two large islands, Upolu and Savaii: the capital, Apia, and the Faleolo International Airport are located on Upolu.

The last sunset of the millennium will take place over the eastern tip of Savaii Island, at Cape Mulinu'u Beach near the rainforest reserve at Falealupo. The sunset is also visible from beaches along the northwest coast such as Fagmalo and Manese.

TRAVEL BRIEF

GETTING THERE The national airline, Polynesian Airlines, operates services to Samoa from New Zealand, Australia, Fiji, Tonga, American Samoa, Hawaii and Los Angeles. Other airlines flying to Samoa include Air New Zealand, Air Pacific and Samoa Air.

ACCOMMODATION Samoa has around 500 hotel rooms, and most of these (including the famous Aggie Greys Hotel in Apia) have been fully booked since 1995. Some budget accommodation may still be available, bookable through Island Hopper Vacations (Samoa), PO Box 2271, Apia,

Samoa Ⓣ 26940 Ⓕ 26941 Ⓔ martel@pactok.peg.apc.org

Another alternative is to stay in a traditional beach *fale*, an open-sided thatched-roof hut containing a mattress and mosquito net. Tanumatiu Beach Fales are located on a beautiful secluded beach just near the sunset point on Savai'i Island. There are no telephones, however, and it is not possible to book in advance.

TOURIST OFFICES Head office: PO Box 2272, Western Samoa Ⓣ 20878 Ⓕ 20886 Ⓔ samoawsvb@talofa.net New Zealand: Auckland Ⓣ 09/ 379 6138. Australia: Sydney Ⓣ 02/ 238 6113. UK: London Ⓣ 0181/392 1838. US: Tahoe City Ⓣ 916/583 0152.

COUNTRY CODE Ⓣ 685

Tonga

Tonga is not prepared to be elbowed aside by Kiribati's decision to move the dateline and has already prepared a detailed list of events for 1999–2000. The kingdom marked the start of the 1000-day countdown to the millennium on April 6, 1997 with a dawn ceremony at the historic **Ha'amonga'a Maui**, attended by His Majesty King Taufa'ahau Tupu the Fourth, ministers, church leaders and hundreds of guests.

The islands are also undergoing a building boom, with over a dozen new properties (including the New Millennium Hotel at Ha'amonga on Tongatapu Island) under construction at a total cost of around US$200 million (£123m). On New Year's Eve there are likely to be huge feasts followed by the *lakalaka* (traditional Tongan dancing). From Tonga you can journey by boat or plane to Samoa for double celebrations.

The wide variety of events planned so far for 1999 include: **New Millennium Festival Week**, Tongatapu (July 1999); **Whale Watch New Millennium Festival**, Vava'u (September 1999); **One-month New Millennium Festival**, Tonga (December 1999); **New Millennium Music Festival** (7-11 December); **New Millennium Eco-Tourism Conference,** and the New Year's Eve celebrations which will include transitional feasting (*tupakapakanava*), cultural shows and a prayer festival.

TRAVEL BRIEF

GETTING THERE Royal Tonga Airlines, Air New Zealand, Polynesian Airlines and Air Pacific link the kingdom with Sydney, Auckland, Fiji, Samoa, Los Angeles and Hawaii.

ACCOMMODATION Resorts, hotels and even some of the guest houses have already received bookings for New Year's Eve 1999, but accommodation is still available.

TOURIST OFFICES Tonga Visitors Bureau, PO Box 37, Nuku'alofa, Kingdom of Tonga Ⓣ 21733 Ⓕ 23507 Ⓔ tvb@candw.to Australia: Sydney Ⓣ 02/519 9700. New Zealand: Auckland Ⓣ 09/634 1519. UK: London Ⓣ 0171/724 5828. US: San Francisco Ⓣ 415/781 0365.

COUNTRY CODE Ⓣ 676

POLAND

P oland's millennium plans revolve around the designation of **Kraków** as a European City of Culture in 2000. Kraków is a popular European short-break destination and a surge of visitors is expected as its medieval beauty is highlighted through cultural events in 2000.

Kraków

For centuries the spirituality of East and West have intermingled in the former royal capital of Kraków, with three major religions – Christianity, Judaism and Islam – co-existing peacefully. This unique spirit of tolerance has given the city its theme for the year 2000, 'Spirituality – Faces of God'. "Kraków commands a singular opportunity to cherish and display all those values, spiritual values which over the centuries have interwoven to create the contemporary image of European culture", say the project's organisers. The project will also aim to provide access to "the other Europe, a world which is receding alongside the declining millennium, but which deserves commemoration for the impact it has had on the civilisation of the Continent".

The **Kraków 2000 Festival** has four main sub-themes: **Images of God** features exhibitions of modern art, eastern icons, western Christian art, and Islamic and Judaic art; **Sounds of Eternity** features religious and secular music; **Places of Mystery** introduces various theatre performances; and **Magical Words** features conferences on art, spirituality and culture. The festival will also feature multimedia performances, workshops, open-air events and special editions of books and CDs. At Easter Kraków will also host the fourth annual **Beethoven Festival**.

Kraków 2000 Cultural Information Centre, Kraków 2000 Festival Bureau, 31-028 Kraków, ul.Sw.Krzya 1 Ⓣ 12/64293487 Ⓕ 6222531.

TRAVEL BRIEF

Poland is still largely unknown as a tourist destination, although Kraków is an essential stop on the rail tour of eastern Europe.

GETTING THERE LOT Polish Airlines operates regular direct flights to Warsaw from New York and Chicago, but there is more choice of timetable and price if you connect via larger European gateways with a range of all major airlines on offer. There are services to Warsaw and Kraków from most European capitals. LOT are the only domestic carriers within Poland.

ACCOMMODATION Accommodation in Poland can be a bit of a lottery, with prices and star-ratings not always reflecting the quality. Most of the top-end hotels still belong to Orbis, although various international chains are heading for the major cities to provide a touch of real cosmopolitan luxury.

TOURIST OFFICES There are two main sources of tourist information in Poland. The PAPT is the state tourism promotion organisation. Orbis, which grew out of the ranks of the old communist structure, is still the country's largest travel agent, tour operator and hotel chain. National: PAPT, ul. Mazowiecka 9, Warsaw ℡ 02/26 62 09; Warsaw: pl. Zamkowy 1/13, 00-262 Warsaw ℡ 02/635 1881; Kraków: ul. Pawia 8, 31-154 Kraków ℡ 12/ 22 60 91 or 22 04 71 UK: London: PAPT: ℡ 0171/580 8811; Polorbis: ℡ 0171/637 4971. US: New York: PAPT: ℡ 212/338 9412; Polorbis: ℡ 212/867 5011; Chicago ℡ 312/236 9013 ⓦ http://www.polandtour.org/

COUNTRY CODE ℡ 48

SPAIN

As a predominantly Catholic country Spain will be celebrating **The Great Jubilee** in churches and cathedrals nationwide, and magnificent processions will also be held during Semana Santa (Easter week) and Corpus Christi (early June). The party-loving Spanish are also unlikely to pass up the opportunity for bigger than usual New Year's Eve celebrations in cities and larger towns.

A major pilgrimage centre for over a thousand years, **Santiago de Compostela** is likely to draw both the faithful and the simply curious in large numbers, especially since 1999 is a **Holy Year**, owing to the fact that the birthday of St James the Apostle falls on a Sunday. The event will be celebrated with a wide-ranging cultural and musical programme. Santiago is also one of the **European Cities of Cultural 2000**.

The Camino de Santiago

After the Ascension, when the apostles began travelling the world as evangelists, St James headed west across the Mediterranean, eventually landing in Hispania on the coast of modern Galicia. His relatively unsuccessful attempt to convert the locals prompted him to return to Palestine, where he became the first Christian martyr in 44 AD. Followers pushed his beheaded body out to sea in an empty boat and angels guided it back to Galicia, where he was reputedly buried on the site of modern Santiago de Compostela. His tomb, however, was lost for several centuries.

Throughout the Moorish invasions of the eighth and ninth centuries, St James is said to have reappeared as a warrior astride a white charger, gallantly slaughtering hundreds of muslim invaders. He became known as Santiago Matamoro (Slayer of Moors) and was adopted as the patron saint of Christian Spain. In 813 a group of shepherds conveniently rediscovered his tomb and almost immediately the area experienced numerous miracles. A massive pilgrimage trade built up until the twelfth century, when almost two million people a year visited the shrine, heading south along five well-tramped paths from all corners of Europe. It was the world's first mass tourist destination, resulting in the world's first guidebook, the *Codex Calixtus*, written by a twelfth-century monk. In 1189 Pope Alexander III declared Santiago a Holy City, third only to Rome and Jerusalem.

Today the pilgrim routes are still clearly defined by the rows of Romanesque churches, chapels and monasteries which mark the way, each roughly ten miles (one day's walk) from the next. The French and northern routes join up near Roncesvalles in the Pyrenees, on the French-Spanish border, to head west across northern Spain. Many people still choose to walk, cycle or ride this last 800km section, wearing the traditional cockle-shell

badge of St James. The Catholic Church still organises cheap pilgrimage accommodation, even supplying a passport, which is stamped at key locations along the way to prove you have made the journey.

☎ 81/54 19 99. The Spanish Tourist Office can provide brochures on the art, architecture and history of the Camino de Santiago (Road to St James), together with general tourist information.

Spain's major capital projects are focused on the Basque capital of Bilbao, which has embarked on an ambitious redevelopment programme, **Bilbao 2000**. The centrepiece of the city's renaissance is the stunning new **Guggenheim Museum** on the waterfront, whose iconoclastic design by architect Frank Gehry attracted worldwide media acclaim when it opened in October 1997. Even a botched attempt by the Basque separatist organisation ETA to blow up the US$100 million (£61m) museum just before the opening ceremony failed to dent the city's enthusiasm for its new post-industrial landmark. "The Guggenheim Bilbao is undoubtedly a scintillating and bombastic design that, in Bilbao, will play much the same role as the opera house in Sydney, Gustave Eiffel's tower in Paris or that of the Great Pyramid of Cheops", wrote one critic. In addition to the museum, the city is also planning a new waterfront development designed by Cesar Pelli, and a new airport.

Compostela 2000, 67 Rua do vilar, 15705 Santiago de Compostela
Ⓣ 81/582525 Ⓔ Compostella2000@coRevia.com

Holy Year 1999, Consellería de Cultura E Comunicación Social, Edificio Administrativo San Caetano, Bloque 3, 15771 Santiago
Ⓣ 81/557246 or 544809 Ⓕ 544830.

SANTIAGO TRAVEL BRIEF

Santiago de Compostela is not geared up for mass tourism and is likely to be swamped during the Holy Year 1999, and during the year 2000 as well.

GETTING THERE There is a small airport with daily flights from the UK, but the nearest major international gateway is Madrid. Many of the world's larger airlines have routes into Madrid.

ACCOMMODATION There are likely to be severe problems finding accommodation in Santiago for much of 1999 and 2000. The magnificent sixteenth-century Hotel de los Reyes Católicos is already full.

TOURIST OFFICES There is no central tourist office for the country. For nationwide telephone information (within Spain) Ⓣ 0901/300 600; Madrid: Duque de Medinacela 2 Ⓣ 01/429 4951 Ⓕ 429 0909; Santiago de

Compostela: Rúa del Villar Ⓣ 81/58 40 81. UK: London Ⓣ 0891/669 920
(premium rate; brochure requests) or 0171/486 8077 (information only). US:
New York Ⓣ 212/265 8822; Los Angeles Ⓣ 213/658 7188 or 658 7192;
Miami Ⓣ 305/358 1992 Ⓦ http://www.spaintour.com/index.html (tourism);
Ⓦ http://www.mec.es/ (cultural sights).

COUNTRY CODE Ⓣ 34

SWITZERLAND

Precise as ever, the Swiss are not planning to celebrate officially until January 1, 2001 with the opening of **Expo
2001** in and around Neuchâtel. There are, however, plans for a
project to build a giant **Wooden Arch** on the slopes of the
famous Mount Rigi, which will open in spring 1999. The
arch, measuring 75m in length, 25m in width and 10m in
height, will remain standing until 2004, after which time it will
be dismantled. Throughout this period it will serve as a location for concerts and plays as well as other cultural activities.

Events

EXPO 2001

May 3–October 29, 2001

The exposition will focus on new ways of communicating
and on the future of transport in the twenty-first century.
Spread over the **Three Lakes District** in western Switzerland, **Expo 2001** will occupy five exhibition sites (called
arteplages), four on the shores of the cities of Bienne,

Neuchâtel, Morat and Yverdonles-Bains, and the fifth a floating platform in the canton of Jura. Twenty high-speed catamarans (each capable of carrying 400 passengers) will shuttle between the sites, which will also be linked to each other via multimedia facilities. Real and virtual voyages of discovery into the past and the future will revolve around different themes in each *arteplage*.

TRAVEL BRIEF

Expo 2001, 4 place de la Gare, Neuchâtel 2002, Switzerland ⓣ 032/726 2001 ⓕ 726 2004 ⓔ info@expo2001.ch ⓦ http://www.expo2001.ch/
COUNTRY CODE ⓣ 41

UNITED STATES

T he vast majority of plans for millennium celebrations in the United States have so far focused on mega-parties, with news that the traditional New Year's Eve celebrations in New York's Times Square will be supplemented by equally flamboyant celebrations in California, Miami and Las Vegas. American travel agencies have also been gearing up in a big way, offering numerous packages for once-in-a-lifetime trips to far-flung corners of the earth.

But travel agents are not the only people to cash in on the celebrations. Hundreds of organisations have registered millennium-related trademarks with the US Federal Trademarks Office. "Everybody and their grandmother now sees the millennium as an economic opportunity", reports Mark Mitten, chair of the **Billennium Organizing Committee**. "It is hard for them to determine what the value of the millennium is [because] it has never happened before [but] the flip side of this unknown brings surety. Because the millennium will only happen once, there could be even more interest and excitement to attract sponsorship." The federal, city and state authorities, adds Mitten, have naturally been more worried about paying for the millennium date change-over in their computer systems than about organising parties.

Another development relating to the celebrations in America has been the dramatic rise in the number of **millennial cults** across the country, ranging from the right-wing militias that gave rise to the Oklahoma City bombing, to New Age groups, to quasi-religious groups who have adopted the imminent arrival of extra-terrestrials as their creed. The most prominent of these was the **Heaven's Gate** cult, who committed mass suicide in March 1997. In view of the cultural dominance of the US in computer technology, it is not surprising to discover that many of these cults are using the Internet to propagate their beliefs.

As an extension of this Internet mania, there has also been a significant increase in idealistic or utopian campaigns, many of them amounting to little more than wishful thinking on a Web site, yet others promoting ideas and philosophies remarkably similar to those of **millennial movements**.

Practically the only building project for the millennium in the US is the new **St Vibiana's Cathedral** in Los Angeles. The original cathedral, one of the few remaining buildings from nineteenth-century Los Angeles, was badly damaged in an earthquake and its proposed demolition caused controversy with conservationists who fought a legal battle to have it restored. However, the Archdiocese opted instead for a new $40 million (£25m) cathedral within the Civic Center, which is being designed by the Spanish architect Jose Rafael Moneo.

Washington DC

"When the millennium finally arrives…none of us will find ourselves suddenly transformed. We won't be trading our earthly jeans and T-shirts for space attire, and we hope that the only bolts of lightning in the sky will be the fireworks that we're planning."

Hillary Rodham Clinton

The year 2000 is the anniversary of a number of symbolic milestones in America's history which will be celebrated in Washington, including the 200-year anniversary of presidents occupying the White House, the 200 year anniversary of the first meeting of Congress in the Capitol, and the 200-year anniversary of the creation of the Library of Congress. Celebrations will focus on these anniversaries as well as on a number of other projects in the White House Millennium Program.

The White House Millennium Program

At a national level, the **White House** launched its own **Millennium Program** in August 1997. Cynics have suggested that this is a belated cobbling together of already existing programmes (a tactic other governments have employed), with the aim of giving a fine millennial polish to the last years of the Clinton administration. But the president has been fascinated by millennial symbolism for quite some time, it has been reported, and was not shy in making 'the bridge to the twenty-first century' one of the key metaphors of his re-election campaign in 1996.

"For centuries, people have wondered what this millennium would bring. Would it signal an Apocalypse or herald a new world, mark a time of decline or a time of renewal. Whatever

the prophecies and forecasts...whatever the hopes and fears,
the millennium is no longer a distant possibility. It has arrived.
We are present at the future, a moment we must now define for
ourselves and for our children."

President Clinton launching the White House Millennium Program,
August 15, 1997

The President's Goals

The White House's three-year programme embraces a number of
activities intended to 'highlight projects that recognise the cre-
ativity and inventiveness of the American people', focusing on
art, culture, scholarship, scientific exploration and technological
discovery. The president is intent on expanding space exploration, preserving the environment and reviving the spirit of citi-
zen service. Of great importance too, is investment in education,
and America plans to connect every classroom and library in the
country to the Internet as soon as possible. A promise has also
been made that government computers will not be hampered by
the Year 2000 'time bomb'. The White House Millennium Program has even launched its own Web site. "We want people of all
ages and walks of life to give us their ideas through the Web
site", said Clinton, with the best local projects to be honoured
with the title Millennium Communities.

The White House Millennium Program will include:

A Festival of American Folklore: This event will be organised by
the Smithsonian Institute, which hopes to involve 200 children
from around the world.

Leadership Project for the Millennium: The National Endowment for the Arts will set out to tell America's story through the
visual arts. Teams of photographers will be sent across the
country to capture their images of America at the turn of the
century.

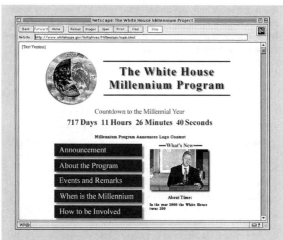

Millennium Stage: Located in the Kennedy Center, this will be in constant use during the Center's year-long arts festival in 2000.

National Archives Preservation Project: A three-year plan has been drawn up for the preservation of treasured national documents, including the Constitution, Bill of Rights and Declaration of Independence.

National Digital Library: The Library of Congress intends to put part of its collection on-line.

NSF 2000: The National Science Foundation campaign is designed to highlight nationwide the importance of science, engineering and mathematics.

White House Lecture Series: Prominent thinkers will be invited to provoke reflection on the past and the future.

White House Millennium Program, 708 Jackson Place, 3rd floor, NW Washington DC 20503 Ⓣ 202/395 7200 Ⓔ millennium@whitehouse.gov Ⓦ http://www.whitehouse.gov/Initiatives/Millennium/index.html

New York City

New York's **Times Square** is synonymous with New Year's Eve in America: the tradition began in 1904 when the owners of One Times Square, the *New York Times*, began holding roof-top parties to usher in the New Year. In 1907 they had the idea of lowering a reflective ball down the 77ft flagpole on top of the building, its descent coinciding with the arrival of midnight. Since then the ball-lowering ceremony has become a potent symbol of New Year's Eve celebrations in America, watched by thousands on the ground and by millions more on television.

In 1997 the **New York Convention and Visitors Bureau** (NYCVB) formed a **Millennium Committee**. Projects planned so far include a series of **Cultural Forums** in the city's museums and elsewhere which will examine issues (such as transportation, education and immigration) that may affect the city in the twenty-first century; another grand New Year's Eve party, **Celebration 2000**; and a mass parade of tall ships, **OpSail 2000**, to be held in July 2000.

The Millennium Committee has also formed a **Millennium Club** for people who want advance information on hotel bookings.

Boston

Boston has already challenged the traditional, booze-soaked image of New Year's Eve with the concept of the **First Night** alcohol-free celebrations, which have already won support in over 170 communities across the US. Clara Wainwright (founder of First Night) and Marilyn Ansem (founder of Mobius) have also instigated the **Millennium Celebration for Boston**, a series of arts-based community projects designed to harness the creative energies of visual and per-

Global Drumming 2000 ...
To Drive Out the Old Millennium &
Welcome the New

A Vision for December 31, 1999

In January, 1999 the word went out on the InterNet and Mickey Hart's website enlarged upon the challenge – create drum circles all over the world to participate in millennium change.

That summer there were hundreds and thousands of workshops – given by Teiko drummers from Osaka to Boston, tabla players from Delhi to Marseilles, Afro-Cuban percussionists from Havana to Kinshasa ... Kids learned to create drums from cardboard boxes and steel barrels; they stretched skins over clay pots ... Artists and musicians collaborated with communities to create huge communal drums in city parks.

forming artists, poets and writers, 'videographers' and others to generate community visions, stage events, and leave a lasting legacy for future generations.

One of their first projects was the **Millennium Mail Art Project**, which first took place in April 1997 at the 1000-day countdown. Artists, writers and others were invited to share their visions with unknown Bostonians by creating a work, copying it, and mailing it out in red envelopes to people picked at random from the telephone directory. Other ideas in the pipeline include an **Inside Out Time Capsule**, which will enable communities to create permanent 'memory walls' containing embedded artifacts, tiles, murals or messages. The walls are to be unveiled throughout December 1999, in conjunction with a series of performance events, **Passport to Here**, involving poetry readings, music, dance, theatre and story-telling intended to capture the nature and history of individual local communities. Other plans include **Community Books**, containing oral histories and photographs, **Millennium Shrines**, and **Millennium Kiosks**, with interactive video touch screens in every neighbourhood.

Millennium Celebration for Boston, c/o Civic Health Institute Community Technology Project Ⓣ 617/825 9660 x 392 Ⓕ 825 0328
Ⓦ http://www.codman.org/boston2000/

Events

California: Mojave Desert

A two-day outdoor event in the **Mojave Desert** over December 31, 1999 and January 1, 2000 is being planned for 'one million spirtually minded people' to join in what they hope is going to be 'the world's largest drumming and chanting circle'. As well as drumming circles and chants there will be 'the largest guided visualisation session in history', music, bonfires and special guests.

Dave Francis, 935 North Beneva Road, Suite 609-12, Sarasota, Florida, Fl 34232. Send $1 for an information pack. Ⓔ thorrrr@hotmail.com
Ⓦ http://www.WhisperedPrayers.com/Millenium?PTML1.html

Party 2000

A nonstop, three-day bash, **Party 2000** will take place on 4000 acres (six square miles) of land in southern California between Palm Springs and the Arizona border. Billing itself as 'The Biggest Concert and Party ever held on Planet Earth', the event has a projected budget of US$1.1 billion (£675m) and the organisers are hoping to attract 2.5 million people. Party 2000 will also feature 'the largest fireworks display ever held in the world'.

The three-day agenda will include big-name bands and live entertainment on 'five of the largest stages ever built' for a one-time event. Booking of bands is expected to begin in mid-1998 and they're hoping for at least fifty top bands.

The venue will be enclosed by a 15ft-high wall and will employ 6500 security staff. It will have four campgrounds (each with 500 cement BBQs) and over 2000 food vendors.

By late 1997 ticket reservations had already passed the 100,000 mark, half from outside the United States. Tickets

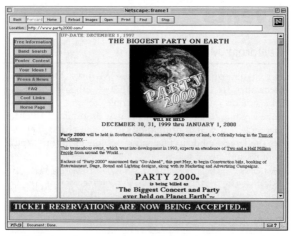

are limited to four per person and the price rises on a sliding scale depending on how early you make a reservation.

Party 2000, 8033 Sunset Blvd, Suite 238, Los Angeles, CA 90046
Ⓣ 1-888/PARTY 2000 or 888/727 8920 Ⓔ mark@party2000.com
Ⓦ http://www.party2000.com/ From mid-1998 details of bands playing at southern California's Party 2000 will be available here as they are announced. You can also e-mail brochure requests and to register for advance tickets. If booked before June 30, 1998 they cost US$330 (£202) per person (US$60/£37 non-refundable deposit), rising to US$445 (£273) if booked before December 31, 1998 (US$85/£52) deposit, US$600 (£368) until June 30, 1999 (must be paid in full), and, if there any tickets left after June 30, 1999, they'll cost US$850 (£521). Credit-card bookings from outside the US are not accepted.

Huntington Beach

The eleventh largest city in California, **Huntington Beach** is planning to hold one of the biggest municipal parties in the state, celebrating its new beachfront amphitheatre, pier plaza, new conference centre and other ambitious developments, all of which should be completed by the year 2000. The three-day event, which will be held between December 31 and January 2, will include fireworks set off from barges along the shoreline, major entertainers rotating between hotels and country clubs, and a citywide Sunday brunch at the beach. Every month in the year 2000 will also be assigned a theme, such as 'Celebrate our Beaches' and 'Salute our Churches'.

Turn of the Century Committee, Suite 2A, 101 Main Street, Huntington Beach, CA 92648 ℡ 714/969 3492.

Florida: Miami's South Beach

Miami might lack New York's historical connection with New Year's celebrations but it is planning to catch up by launching its own large-scale events, leading up to a mega-party at the millennium. "Last New Year's Eve it was 10° with wind chill in Times Square...and 70° with a warm sea breeze on South Beach. Where would you rather be?" ask the promoters of '**New Year on South Beach**'. Ideas being mooted include 'a nonstop, multimedia extravaganza', with huge sound, light and video towers placed at intervals along the beach, alternating with stages for entertainment, live music, and 'the hottest DJs and fashion shows'.

At midnight a fireworks display, synchronised to music, will be launched from barges off the beach.

The city is still finalising its plans for what it says will be an 'outrageous, outstanding, fantastic' celebration.

Sobe Productions, 2637 East Atlantic Blvd, Suite 170, Pompano Beach, FL 33062 ℡ 800/664-SOBE Ⓔ hitthebeach@sobenewyears.com Ⓦ http://www.sobenewyears.com/

Massachusetts: First Night 2000, Boston

First Night has its origins in Boston in 1976, when a group of artists had the novel idea of hosting an alcohol-free cele-

Pedalling Odyssey

Los Angeles to Los Angeles via the world, 366 days, 20,000 miles, 54 countries. Billed as the 'ultimate cycling adventure', Odyssey 2000 starts on January 1, 2000. Averaging 77 miles a day, the ride will be supported by a mobile bike shop, canteen, portable showers and toilets, medical facilities and, for those weary limbs, a masseur. So far, Odyssey has 330 people signed up to ride, including an 81-year-old woman from Florida who will be accompanied by her daughter, son-in-law and two grandchildren. And the cost? Just $US36,000 (£23,000), which includes transportation on non-ridable sectors, with the bonus that you get to keep your special Odyssey 2000 bike (if it, and you, survive the journey).

Odyssey 2000, 200 Lake Washington Blvd, Suite 101, Seattle, WA. 98122-6540 Ⓣ 8000/433 0528 or 206/322 4102 Ⓕ 322 4509 Ⓦ http://www.cortland.com/bike_expo/kneeland.html

bration on New Year's Eve revolving around shared artistic experiences. Supported by local businesses and government, **First Night Boston** set out to showcase the visual and performing arts with a diverse, high-quality programme that was accessible and affordable to all. It quickly became a success, with annual attendances in excess of 1.5 million people.

Since then this tradition has spread across small towns and big cities alike. Between 150 and 170 festivals have taken place in recent years in locations as far apart as Santa Cruz, California to Tampa, Florida, as well as in several Canadian cities. In Hawaii First Night was inaugurated in 1990 under the slogan 'Arts, Not Alcohol' with 40,000 people in attendance, a figure that had increased to more than 120,000 by 1996. A major bonus of this project has been the reduction in traffic fatalities in Honolulu on New Year's Eve.

Each First Night is unique. In New York, they've had dance

parties, jazz performances and stand-up comedy; in Tampa, roving entertainers, a 'resolution tree', art mazes, and outdoor music; in Calgary, over 100 artists have taken part in performances at twenty locations; in Ocean City, they've staged magicians, dancers, bands and more; in Boston, ice sculptures and a grand procession are regular features. The emphasis is on wholesome, family entertainment, normally culminating in a firework display.

Most of these First Night organisations are currently busy making plans for **First Night 2000**.

First Night Inc., 20 Park Plaza, Suite 927, Boston MA 02116 Ⓣ 617/542 1399 Ⓕ 426 9531 Ⓦ http://www.firstnight.org/ Ⓔ fnteam@firstnight.org

New York State: Celebration 2000

This series of events based at the **Jacob Javits Convention Center** will include a **Twentieth-Century Collectibles Exhibition** (December 20, 1999–January 1, 2000), as well as a gala New Year's Eve party at a location overlooking the Hudson River. A percentage of the proceeds will go to the Save the Children fund.

Jacob Javits Convention Center, 655 West 34th Street, New York, NY 10001-1188 Ⓣ 212/216 2176 Ⓕ 216 4099.

Times Square 2000

The carefully choreographed countdown to the New Year in **Times Square** begins with the lighting up of the ball at its highest point on the flagpole at dusk. The rhinestone-clad aluminium ball, which weighs 500 pounds and is 6ft in diameter, is equipped with 144 glitter strobe lights, 180 halogen lamps and a 10,000 watt internal lamp. At one minute to midnight a laser lights up the ball as it begins its descent down the flagpole and, as the digital clocks on screens around the square mark the midnight moment, tonnes of confetti floats down from the building around the square.

Search lights, laser lights and spotlights scan the crowds as the fireworks go off in southern Central Park.

On New Year's Eve 1999 the theme for the event is 'Times Square 2000 – The Global Celebrations at the Crossroads of the World'. Giant video screens will be positioned around the square, broadcasting footage of celebrations taking place around the world, beginning with Fiji at 7am EST.

Visitor Information Hotline Ⓣ 212/354-0003

Ⓦ http://www.time-square.org/newyear.htm Schedule of events.

Ⓦ http://www.yahoo.com/promotions/newyears/

Live cybercasts from the event. Ⓦ http://www.times-square.org/

Facts about New Year's Eve in Times Square, including a complete schedule of events.

Texas: March for Jesus

June 10, 2000

The organisers of the **Jesus March 2000** are hoping that up to 30 million people in 2000 cities, towns and villages will take part in a procession of prayer and worship.

March for Jesus, PO Box 3216, Austin, TX

Ⓔ 76423.2504@compuserve.com

Meet in the Middle Festival

December 30, 1999–January 1, 2000

The organisers of the **Meet in the Middle Festival** are planning for people from all over the States to converge somewhere in southeast Texas for a three-day outdoor festival of music. Every style will be catered for, from jazz to reggae to country, hip-hop and rock.

Meet in the Middle, 1231 Dickinson Dr PT 1220, Coral Gables, FL 33146.

Washington State: Seattle

The **Spirit of 2000** committee has been formed to co-ordinate events across Washington state. In Seattle these will include parades, fireworks out on the city's waterway, **Puget Sound** and from the top of the famous **Space Needle**, and a 'pray-for-peace' vigil.

Spirit of 2000, 1904 Third Ave 700, Seattle, WA 98101 Ⓣ / Ⓕ 206/623 5967 Ⓦ http://www.spirit2000.com/

TRAVEL BRIEF

With multiple time zones to choose from between Hawaii and New England, the US has plenty of time to party and intends to take full advantage of it. There are vast beach parties in Miami, Florida, and Huntington Beach, California, while the California desert is hosting a gigantic pop-festival-cum-party. In New York, of course, the traditional Times Square countdown is aiming to become *the* event. Other celebrations are springing up across the entire country.

GETTING THERE Ground-level travel within the US is only really practical over relatively small distances as passenger trains are infrequent, except on the northeastern seaboard, and buses take a very long time. Most people, both American and foreign, choose to fly. The US has probably the busiest air network in the world, with flights to every destination, both domestic and international, provided by two giants, Delta and United. Both are prepared to add some additional flights should it prove necessary, but the decision will not be taken until 1999. In New York City, there is adequate public transport and a car is a liability. Elsewhere you will probably want to hire a car, and availability may be a real problem. Book as soon as possible.

ACCOMMODATION Some luxury hotels in New York, Miami and Los Angeles are booked up, as are the most romantic restaurants. "The biggest millennium myth right now is that New York City is sold out", says the NYCVB.

"We've hardly even begun to take bookings." Most hotels will not begin taking reservations until mid-1998 or early 1999. The first booking for New Year's Eve 1999 was made in 1983, by a man from upstate New York who contacted the Marriott Marquis, which is in a prime position on Times Square when building work began on the hotel. His foresight has been rewarded by a complimentary suite for the night. The Seattle Space Needle restaurant has been fully booked since 1991. Major tourist attractions such as Disney World are also full, with long waiting lists. If you want to spend the millennium in luxury in the US, look for the remote, out-of-town resorts and book as soon as possible. Florida, southern California and New York, all awash with more ordinary hotel beds, are used to handling mass events and don't see the millennium as anything out of the ordinary. Sensible advance booking is advised but there should be enough accommodation for most, if not all.

NYCVB, Two Columbus Circle, New York, NY 10019
Ⓣ 1-800/NYC-VISIT (US and Canada); Ⓣ 212/397 8222

TOURIST OFFICES Membership of the Millennium Club costs US$20 (£12). Contact: NYC Millennium Club, NYCVB, 810 Seventh Avenue, New York, NY 10019 Ⓣ 212/941 9527; Los Angeles: 633 West 5th St, Ste 6000, Los Angeles CA 90071 Ⓣ 213/236 2343 Ⓕ 236 2395; Miami: 701 Brickell Ave, Ste 2700, Miami, FL 33131 Ⓣ 305/539 3063 Ⓕ 539 3113. UK: California: ABC California, PO Box 35, Abingdon, Oxon OX14 4SP (send £2/US$3 for a brochure pack; there is no public information telephone line); New York: there is no tourist office, but the Port Authority (handling all transport into the city) does have some information Ⓣ 0171/439 0020; Miami: Ⓣ 0171/439 1216
Ⓦ (California): http://gocalif.ca.gov
Ⓦ (Miami): http://www.miamiandbeaches.com
Ⓦ (New York): http://WWW.NYCVISIT.COM

COUNTRY CODE Ⓣ 1

THE MILLENNIUM

CONTEXTS

Some Millennial History

Preoccupations with the end of the world (the apocalypse) and universal transformation are clear manifestations of the millennial myth, a defining archetype in western consciousness which has run like a thread through the beliefs of cults, prophets, New Age visionaries and doomsday sects over the last 2000 years. But where did it all start – and what lies in store for the year 2000? Read on . . .

The Roots of Apocalypse

Belief in the apocalypse has its roots in the ancient teachings of **Zoroaster**, an Iranian prophet who lived around 1500 BC. Zoroaster's vision was of a wise and powerful God, **Ahura Mazda**, who was plagued by an evil twin, **Angra Mainyu**. The prophet held the theory that the long and arduous battle between these two would eventually result in victory for Ahura Mazda. The complete transformation of the world would then occur, leading to a universal resurrection and the elevation to perfect immortality of believers. In other words, Zoroaster more or less invented the notion of heaven and hell.

Zoroastrianism is thought to be the world's first eschatological faith – that is, there can be no return to a former paradise, but a total transformation into another state. The historical cycle of time effectively ends.

The Book of Daniel

Zoroaster's prophecies had an important influence on early Judaism, which is most apparent in the **Book of Daniel** (written around 168 BC). This particular text marked a decisive shift away from previous Jewish prophecies by suggesting that there would indeed be a final cataclysm, a battle between good and evil, and a resurrection of the dead followed by a golden age.

A crucial concept in the Book of Daniel is that salvation is imminent, and it is this shared belief in the imminent arrival of the apocalypse that has become the hallmark of millenarian movements throughout history. Although Daniel was cryptic about the actual date ('a time, two times, and half a time'), he left enough numerical clues to generate speculation for over 2000 years, and his words are still being scrutinised today by those who believe that the year 2000 heralds the apocalypse and/or a new dawn.

The Revelation of St John the Divine

Just over fifty years after the death of Jesus, Nero launched the first great persecution of Christians, which continued throughout the reign of the Emperor Titus Flavius Domitianus. It was around this time (between 65 and 100 AD) that a believer called John (his exact identity is uncertain) was exiled to the Greek island of Patmos, where he wrote the hugely influential and enigmatic **Book of Revelation**. "I was in the Spirit on the Lord's Day", he recorded, "and heard behind me a great voice, as of a trumpet, saying 'I am Alpha and Omega, the first and the last: and, what thou seest, write it in a book, and send it unto the seven churches which are in Asia'" (Rev 1: 10–11).

The dramatic vision that enveloped him unfolded as a series of bizarre images – beasts with multiple eyes and wings, locusts 'with the hair of women and the teeth of lions', great dragons, lakes burning with brimstone, glass seas, and 'foul spirits like frogs' – which take on a hallucinatory quality as the whole of creation is sucked into a vortex of destruction and renewal.

The imagery of the Book of Revelation owes more to religious cults of the Middle East, Greece and Egypt than it does to the conventions of early Christian writings, but its crucial significance lies in its depiction of the pattern of events leading

up to the **Second Coming of Christ** and the **Last Judgement**.

Although many of Jesus's followers lived in daily expectation of the apocalypse, after his death the focus shifted to the Second Coming, which Jesus had implied would occur in their own lifetimes. When this failed to happen some explanation was needed, and the Book of Revelation adequately served this purpose. For persecuted Christians it not only reiterated the scale of the reward that awaited them in the eternal kingdom, but also partially explained the delay in Christ's Second Coming by revealing the full horror of the battle between good and evil which was still taking place.

Although John was not the first to suggest that the 'end-time' sequence had begun, it is largely due to his writings that the notion of an imminent apocalypse gained widespread currency. His cosmology represents the quintessential millennial myth, a vision that explains the death and rebirth of the world.

The Seven Seals

Part of John's vision describes a door opening into heaven to reveal a throne surrounded by 24 elders, clothed in white with crowns of gold. 'There was a rainbow round about the throne' and 'out of the throne proceeded lightnings and thunderings and voices' (Rev 4: 3, 5). The Holy One holds in his hand a book with seven seals, which 'no man in heaven, nor in earth, neither under the earth, can open' (Rev 5: 4), but a lamb with seven horns and seven eyes (signifying Christ) appears and takes the book. As the first four seals are broken the Four Horsemen of the Apocalypse appear, the last of whom is Death. 'Hell followed with him. And power was given unto them over the fourth part of the earth, to kill with sword, and with hunger, and with death, and with the beasts of the earth' (Rev 6: 8).

With the opening of the fifth seal all those martyred for Christianity arise. With the sixth, 'lo, there was a great earthquake; and the sun became black as sackcloth of hair, and the moon became as blood; and the stars of heaven fell unto earth. And the heaven departed as a scroll when it is rolled together; and every mountain and island were moved out of their places' (Rev 6: 12–14). Thus the Wrath of God gives a foretaste of things to come, whilst the chosen 144,000 who are to be saved are marked by four angels of the wind.

With the seventh seal there is a temporary peace until seven angels blow their trumpets to unleash the real apocalypse. The world is subjected to hail and fire mingled with blood. Mountains are cast into the sea, the star Wormwood falls from the sky, the sun and the moon are dimmed, and unbelievers are tormented by scorpions and beasts arising from a fiery pit.

In the midst of the deluge, a pregnant woman appears, accompanied by a seven-headed red dragon. As the woman gives birth the dragon tries to devour the baby, but it is defeated by St Michael. The dragon (who is Satan) appears in a new form, a beast rising out of the sea, 'having seven heads and ten horns, and upon his horns ten crowns' (Rev 13: 1). This creature is the Antichrist, the Beast of the Apocalypse, 'and his number is six hundred threescore and six' (Rev 13: 18).

The chosen ones ascend to Mt Sion with the lamb and, as Babylon falls, they witness the torment of the infidels. A white horse appears, mounted by a figure 'clothed with a vesture dipped in blood, and his name is the Word of God' (Rev 19: 13). He wages war on the beast and his followers, and Satan is cast into a bottomless pit and bound for a thousand years.

The Importance of Revelation

John's account of the Seven Seals heralds the beginning of Christ's **millennial reign**. 'And I saw a new heaven and a new earth: for the first heaven and first earth were passed away' (Rev 21: 1). A new Jerusalem descends from heaven, and all suffering is eradicated: 'And God shall wipe away the tears from their eyes, and there shall be no more death, neither sorrow, nor crying, neither shall there be any more pain, for the former things are passed away' (Rev 21: 4). The delights of the new Jerusalem, with its walls of jasper, streets of gold and twelve pearly gates, are described in some detail.

John ends with a warning to anyone who might consider meddling with his manuscript: 'If any man shall add unto these things, God shall add unto him the plagues that are written in this book' (Rev 21: 18).

The Book of Revelation has had, and continues to have, "a greater effect on human behaviour in the western world than any other single piece of writing", claims one millennial commentator. "It is perhaps the most powerful source of utopian hope in western civilisation", says another. Certainly, the Book's concepts and images – the Battle of Armageddon, the Four Horsemen of the Apocalypse, and the Great Beast whose number is 666 – have occupied a firm position in the iconography of western consciousness through the centuries.

The Montanist Heresy

By the second century the Christian church was well established and, although there was still speculation on the Second Coming, the church hierarchy was able to gloss over this issue in the interests of maintaining the status quo. But the situation of relative calm was soon disturbed with the arrival of the first heretical apocalyptic cult, the **Montanists**.

Founded in Phrygia, Asia Minor, in the second century AD, the sect was led by a Christian convert called **Montanus**, together with two priestesses, Priscilla and Maximilla. Speaking in strange tongues, the group prophesied that the new Jerusalem was about to descend to earth in the region of Phrygia, and they encouraged Christians to abandon their villages and follow them to the appointed place. When the 'new heaven and new earth' failed to materialise, Montanus and his priestesses are thought to have committed suicide. The sect survived without them for another 700 years, however, spreading throughout Asia Minor, despite condemnation by the church.

The Montanists are significant not only because they represented the first heretical challenge to the orthodox church but also because they were one of the first clearly defined examples of what anthropologists call **millenarian movements**. Often arising in times of social and cultural upheaval, millenarian movements thrive on the promise of a better life, a utopia lurking around the corner. The fact that they flourish as a result of discontent with the established order often places these movements in conflict with the dominant culture. Frenzied behaviour, coupled with mass migration to the spot where they will await the new millennium, is also a characteristic of apocalyptic cults that has manifested itself throughout the centuries.

Medieval Millennialism

Was the year 1000 marked by a sense of impending apocalypse? Historians differ, but the popular view is that the masses did succumb to some form of millennial fever. In his book *Millennium Prophecies,* Stephen Skinner writes, "For a few short months in 999 AD people could talk of nothing else but the Second Coming. In Europe generally a sort of mass hysteria took hold as the year end approached. This atmosphere led to some astonishing happenings. Some men forgave each other their debts; husbands and wives rashly confessed infidelities; convicts were released from prison; poachers made a truce with their liege lords....December saw fanaticism reach new heights as communities attempted to rid their area of the ungodly."

Damian Thompson disagrees with this account, however, in *The End of Time.* "The 'Terrors of the Year 1000' appear to be a romantic invention of sixteenth-century historians", he asserts. "The main reason for disbelieving accounts of apocalpytic expectations in the year 1000 is that at the time the majority of the population had no notion of what year it was anyway."

The Middle Ages were, nonetheless, ripe for outbreaks of millennialism. It was a time of social turmoil which saw whole populations suffer wars, famines, plagues and invasions, as well as economic and social dislocation as international trade routes opened up and people began to travel more widely. At the same time, the notion of an imminent end to the world was central to popular religious beliefs. The stage was set for the emergence of numerous apocalyptic prophets and messianistic cults.

The Crusades

In the first millennium after Christianity the established church tended to make light of 'end-time' beliefs, and apart from a few isolated examples such as the Montanists, there is little evidence of any powerful millenarian movement. But from the eleventh century onwards the church hierarchy began to turn millenarian beliefs to their own advantage. This new strategy began with the holy wars that became known as the **Crusades**.

The 200-year period of the Crusades began in 1095. The aim of the western European kingdoms was to wrest control of Jerusalem and other sacred sites in the Holy Land from the Muslim powers, and the Christian church mounted at least eight major expeditions to this end before it was finally expelled from Syria in 1291. The millennial myth was used by some clerics to justify the campaign of aggression. The seizure of Jerusalem was judged a prelude to the arrival of the Antichrist; its overthrow would hasten the final Battle of Armageddon.

But whilst the church had envisaged well-disciplined and well-equipped armies of chivalric knights in its ranks, the call to liberate the Holy Land also took root amongst the peasantry. At the end of the eleventh century northern Europe had been through a succession of floods, droughts, famines and plagues, and since these were precisely the sort of prophetic 'signs' that were taken to herald the beginning of the end, the masses formed their own ragged army of crusaders and began travelling across Europe.

This was the **People's Crusade**, a chance for many to escape their intolerable lives and seek salvation in Jerusalem. "Gradually, the image of real Jerusalem became confused with the perfect New Jerusalem of scripture; rumours circulated of a miraculous realm where common people lived like princes", writes Damian Thompson, who describes it as "classic millenarianism".

The Third Age

During the thirteenth century, millenarian movements, nourished by the mass anxieties of the time, experienced vigorous growth throughout Europe. This period also saw the emergence of a new kind of millenarianism which was to prove highly influential in later centuries. The latest prophetic voice was that of **Joachim of Fiore**, a Calabrian abbot who had a vision (sometime between 1190 and 1195) of a complex pattern underlying history which revealed humanity's progress through three successive stages: the **Age of the Father**, the **Age of the Son** and the **Age of the Spirit**.

Anchoring the three different ages within the numerology of the Bible, Joachim reckoned that the **Third Age** was due to arrive around 1260 and that it would be a golden age of love, freedom and joy which would last for a thousand years until the Last Judgement. The prevailing orthodoxy at the time was that the Kingdom of God was already present, and by declaring that utopia had yet to occur within history, Joachim was inadvertently subverting the church.

The abbot's vision had an important influence on European mythology and, centuries later, its central tenets surfaced in secular revolutionary movements such as **Marxism** and the idea of the **Third Reich** – the Nazi concept of the glorious thousand-year reign.

Roving Flagellants

Penitential **self-flagellation** was common in monasteries from the eleventh century onwards, but in the thirteenth century it came to be embraced by the masses – amid millennial overtones. Earliest demonstrations occurred in Italy, where priests bearing sacred candles and banners led processions from town to town. Arriving at a church, the flagellants would whip themselves for hours on end using leather scourges armed with iron spikes. Eventually, many thousands joined in this practice as the processions moved further across the countryside.

Mass **flagellant movements** also sprang up in southern Germany and France and continued to reappear for the next 200 years. In Germany this concept of contrition evolved into a more militant messianic movement, with leaders urging the populace to disobey (and in some cases stone to death) the clergy and appropriate the church's wealth. The flagellants also massacred numerous Jewish communities, fuelled by rumours that the Jews had caused the outbreak of the Black Death by poisoning the drinking water.

Doomsday Cults

The flagellants were one of the first millenarian groups to preach armed resistance to the church. Founded in 1260, the **Apostolic Brethren** believed that they alone were the beneficiaries of God's word and that the pope and all his cardinals would soon be destroyed in a final conflagration. Led by **Fra Dolcino**, the Brethren retreated to the Alps to arm themselves for the decisive battle, but they were eventually defeated at Monte Rebello in 1307.

The movement's destruction was one of the first examples of a **doomsday cult** locked into a self-fulfilling prophecy that eventually led to their own demise, a pattern of self-destructive milllenarian behaviour that has continued until the present day (the bloodbath at Waco in 1993 is a classic example). "Of all the apocalyptic mutations, none has appeared with such tragic regularity as the small group which hides behind fortifications in expectation of glorious deliverance from a cataclysmic onslaught by the forces of evil", writes Damian Thompson. "The believers jump the gun by taking up arms themselves, and the onslaught materialises."

The Doctrine of Free Love

Self-flagellation was not the only trend in medieval millenarianism veering towards the socially dysfunctional. For nearly five centuries a belief known as the **Heresy of the Free Spirit** appeared in various guises (it was also known as 'Spiritual Liberty' and the 'Spirit of Freedom') throughout Europe. Adherents believed that they had obtained absolute perfection and were not only therefore incapable of sin, but expected to do things that were forbidden. In Antwerp, one adept of the Free Spirit, **Willem Cornelis**, preached that since poverty abolished all sins the poor could indulge in sex as much as they liked. Cornelis himself was said to have been 'wholly given up to lust', and it took the church authorities more than twenty years to try and stamp out his promiscuous beliefs in the city. Elsewhere, the Brethren of the Free Spirit preyed on lonely widows or unmarried women in the towns and cities.

Predictably enough, the doctrine of spiritual emancipation through eroticism proved highly popular. Similar beliefs were found amongst the **Adamites**, a millenarian cult in fifteenth-century Bohemia who preached free love and 'danced naked around camp fires'. These states of mystical ecstacy were an essential part of a belief in the return to a state of innocence, of perfection on earth.

Nostradamus

Born in Provence in 1503, **Michel de Nostradame** is the most famous prophet of the last thousand years, and his predictions have been studied avidly for the last four and a half centuries. He was known simply as Nostradamus (the Latinised version of his name), and his predictive talents were encouraged by his grandfather, who was physician to King René of Provence. Having shown an early aptitude for astrology and maths, Nostradamus was sent to study the arts in Avignon, but upset his teachers by defending astrology and the theories of Copernicus. He then studied medicine at Montpellier and became well known as a plague doctor before losing his own wife and children to the Black Death when he was just 34.

Nostradamus wandered in self-imposed exile in Italy and southern Europe, the tragedy turning his energies inwards to the occult for the next ten years, a time during which he is said to have developed his prophetic vision. In 1544 he returned to Provence, married a rich widow and devoted himself whole-heartedly to the predictive arts. He began writing an annual almanac and was sufficiently encouraged by its success to embark on what was to become his most famous work, the seven-volume *Centuries*, intended as a future history of the world.

In 1556 Nostradamus predicted the death of Henry II of France in a jousting accident, which drew him to the attention of the queen, **Catherine de Medici**. In 1559 Henry II was duly killed as foreseen, making Nostradamus the talk of the courts of Europe. Crowds burned effigies of him before the Inquisitors, and he was only rescued from death by Catherine, who later encouraged Charles IX to elevate him to the status of Counselor and Physician in Ordinary.

Just eighteen months later, Nostradamus died as he himself had prophesied: 'On his return from the embassy, the King's gift put in place. He will do nothing more. He will be gone to God. Close relatives, friends, brothers by blood will find him completely dead near the bed and the bench.'

Nostradamus's *Centuries* comprises a series of 942 four-line quatrains. Written in a combination of French, Latin, Greek and Provençal, the poetic and obscure nature of the prophecies has proved a fruitful source of material for interpreters, who have been able to read into them whatever they want. Nostradamus consciously made them enigmatic, jumbling time sequences and historical allusions to protect himself against potential repercussions.

Century 3, Quatrain 95

This particular quatrain is said by commentators, among them Stefan Paulus, to have predicted the fall of communism:

The Law of More people
will be seen to fall:
After a different one a
good deal more seductive:
Dnieper first will fall:
Through gifts and language to
another more attractive.

'More' as used here is said to refer to **Sir Thomas More**, who published his *Utopia* when Nostradamus was a student, the inference being that utopia was an allegory for communism. Democracy is seen as a 'different one' (political system) which replaced communism because it was 'a good deal more seductive'. The **Dnieper** runs through Kiev, the capital of the Ukraine, which was one of the first breakaway states from the USSR. And the transition came about peacefully, 'through gifts' (pledges of aid) and 'language' (diplomacy).

Century 10, Quatrain 72

Dozens of volumes have been written on Nostradamus's enigmatic quatrains, all of them offering different interpretations, but most scholars seem to agree that the prophet's most compelling prediction concerning the millennium is Century 10, Quatrain 72:

The year 1999,
the seventh month,
From the sky will come
a great King of Terror;
Resuscitating the great
King of the Mongols,
Before and after Mars
to reign happily.

It is one of the very few quatrains to mention a specific date but, despite this, some argue that the original French word, 'sept' might be short for September. The 'great King of Terror' is thought to imply the imminent arrival of a comet, which would collide with the planet, or indeed a nuclear war. The reference to the **King of the Mongols**, Genghis Khan, is interpreted as pointing the finger at northwest China, but there again, others maintain that the reference alludes to an advanced alien civilisation which will be able to clone Genghis Khan's cells to resurrect the Antichrist. Some commentators have also made much of the proximity of this date to a major planetary alignment which will take place in August 1999, when the last solar eclipse of the century will be followed by a Grand Cross of the planets in the fixed signs of the zodiac (Taurus, Leo, Scorpio and Aquarius) which correspond to the Four Horsemen of the Apocalypse in John's Revelation.

The only prediction that is 100 percent certain is that books on Nostradamus will continue to be churned out well into the next millennium.

Nineteenth-century Prophets

Millenarian movements have always had to deal with the consequences of their own blunders as the date set for the apocalypse passes by uneventfully. In medieval Europe theological obfuscation was often deployed to gloss over the disappointment, but in later centuries this trick became more difficult, especially once the arrival of newspapers ensured that predictions of a Second Coming achieved much wider publicity, and that these 'false profits' were mercilessly exposed to public ridicule.

Joanna Southcott

The daughter of a Devonshire peasant, **Joanna Southcott** began prophesying in 1792 and drew a large following owing to her increasingly accurate predictions concerning events such as the French Revolution. In 1802 she began annointing the 144,000 people who were to enjoy Christ's millennial reign, among them many clergymen. In 1814 the 64-year old virgin became convinced that she had been impregnated with the Holy Ghost and would give birth to the child 'Shiloh', a new Christ-figure who would redeem the world. Seventeen of the twenty-one doctors who examined her pronounced that she was probably or definitely pregnant, and dozens of people camped outside her London home awaiting the event. She died in 1815, ten days after the baby was due, and an autopsy revealed no evidence of pregnancy, nor could it establish the cause of death.

A later Southcottian follower, **Helen Exeter**, founded the **Panacea Society** and sealed Southcott's writings in a box that had once belonged to her. The Society, which still exists today, believes that opening the box will usher in a new era, but that it must be opened in the presence of all the bishops of the Church of England – a gathering that is highly improbable, despite newspaper advertisements placed by the Society demanding that the event takes place.

Charles Hindley and the Mother Shipton Prophecies

Although they first appeared in the mid-fifteenth century, the prophecies of **Mother Shipton** achieved widespread popularity in the nineteenth century when an editor named **Charles Hindley** decided to publish the predictions, adding a few of his own along the way. Numerous legends surround the birth of Mother Shipton (Ursula Southiel 1488–1561), including one that she was born in a cave after her mother had been impregnated by a superhuman being. She became famous as a seer whilst in her twenties, correctly predicting **Henry VIII's invasion of France** in 1513, the destruction of the **Spanish Armada** and the **Great Fire of London** in 1666.

The Millerites

The **Millerites**, a millennial cult that took hold in Boston and New York in the mid-nineteenth century, was founded by **William Miller**, a farmer who began scrutinising the books of Daniel and Revelation and who became convinced that the Second Coming would occur during the year 1843. His preaching attracted a large following, particularly after the appearance of a meteor in 1833 which was interpreted as a signal that the time was nigh. A Boston pastor founded several newspapers (including one called *Signs of the Times*) to promote Miller's ideas, which fell on fertile ground in New York State as floods and crop failures exacerbated the effects of the depression, encouraging 50,000–100,000 people to join the movement.

Miller announced the date for the Second Coming as sometime between March 21, 1843 and March 21, 1844. When the first date came and went without incident, it was described as 'The Great Disappointment', and many followers abandoned the movement. But others decided a recalculation was necessary, and hit upon October 22, 1844 as the second plausible date. Members moved to the hilltops to await the great event, and when nothing occurred, the disappointment was overwhelming: 'we wept and wept until the day dawned', said one disciple.

Thus was born the comic stereotype of the doomsday prophet, surrounded by his followers 'staring up in disbelief at an empty sky'. It was the first time in history that an apocalyptic movement had become the laughing stock of the public.

The Ghost Dancers

Millennial prophecies found a receptive audience amongst Native Americans, eager for a redemptive vision as they witnessed the erosion of their culture, loss of their lands, and social upheaval caused by the introduction of alcohol. One of the most celebrated movements was the **Sioux Ghost Dance**, inspired by the visions of the shaman **Wovoka** in 1886. Wovoka foresaw a cataclysm that would overwhelm white civilisation, bring back the Plains buffalo, restore Indian culture, and resurrect those they had lost.

The Sioux were urged to dance nonstop for five whole days in an attempt to bring about the impending apocalypse, scheduled for the spring of 1891. "When the earth shakes at the coming of the new world, do not be afraid; it will not hurt you", claimed Wovoka. The Sioux dressed themselves in 'ghost shirts' which they believed had the magical ability to protect them against the bullets of white troops, but in 1890 nearly 300 men, women and children were massacred during the battle at Wounded Knee Creek.

Another Native American messianic movement was the **Earth Lodge**, who predicted that floods and earthquakes would swallow up white culture. Adherents built large, circular underground chambers where they could shelter when the apocalypse arrived.

Jehovah's Witnesses

Founded by **Charles Taze Russell** (1852–1916) in Pittsburgh in 1872, the **Jehovah's Witnesses** are one of the best known of Christian millennial cults, largely due to their door-to-door evangelism. Witnesses believe that the Battle of Armageddon is imminent and that it will cleanse the earth for the arrival of the Kingdom of God, which will last for a thousand years.

The date Russell first predicted for the establishment of the Kingdom of God was 1874, and when this failed he settled on October 1914. This date was then reinterpreted as the year in which Christ was enthroned in Heaven, and the timetable for Armageddon was reset to 1975. It was then revised many more times until, in 1995, the church's journal,

The Watchtower, pronounced that no more dates would be set.

Jehovah's Witnesses must refuse to serve in the armed forces or vote. Estimates vary as to their numbers, which are thought to be anything between four and eleven million people worldwide.

Edgar Cayce

Known as 'the sleeping prophet', **Edgar Cayce** (1877–1945) has been called America's Nostradamus. He predicted a number of events with a high degree of accuracy – and many more that were completely wrong. During consultations he would lie down to sleep, allowing his 'inner light' to channel communications, claiming to remember nothing when he woke. Just before the Wall Street crash in early 1929 he advised clients not to invest in stocks and shares, predicting a 'downward movement of long duration'.

His followers claim that he also foresaw the downfall of communism, both world wars, the assassination of President Kennedy, and independence for India and Israel. Other less successful predictions included California falling into the sea in 1969, the emergence of new islands in the Caribbean, and China becoming a 'new cradle for Christianity'.

In 1934 Cayce gave a trance reading in which he predicted that there would be a shift in the earth's axis in 1999, leading to widespread natural disasters, as well as World War III. The year 2000, his followers believe, will see the Second Coming of Christ and the advent of the New Age. His well-documented predictions are maintained by the **Association for Research and Enlightenment**, based at his former home in Virginia.

Mormons

Mormons are members of the **Church of Jesus Christ of Latter-Day Saints**, a millennial group often confused with the Jehovah's Witnesses, since both proselytise on doorsteps. Mormons hold firm beliefs in the imminent end of the world – members are required to stockpile a year's supply of food, clothes and emergency supplies in preparation for the approaching Armageddon.

The church was founded by **Joseph Smith** (1805–44), who is said to have had his first divine revelation at the age of 14 when he went into the woods and met two figures, God and Jesus, who told him to have nothing to do with established religions. Later, an angel called Moroni appeared and instructed him to translate a secret history of North America, written on golden tablets, conveniently located on a hillside near his home. This became the **Book of Mormon**.

The Book of Mormon claims that America was discovered by various Hebrew tribes around 600 BC, some of whom perished, but others of whom survived internecine wars to become the nucleus of the people who were later known as Red Indians. The Book also rejects the conventional Christian doctrine of the one true God.

After it was published, Smith established the Church of Jesus Christ of the Latter-Day Saints and attracted a considerable following. But he also met with fierce local opposition from the established churches, and the 'saints' (as Mormons refer to themselves) were chased out of Vermont. They went first to Ohio, then to Missouri, then Illinois, and finally to Utah, where they founded **Salt Lake City** – still the worldwide headquarters of the movement.

In 1844 Smith announced that he was running for the US presidency and opposition reached fever pitch. After smashing up a newspaper office hostile to the Mormons, Smith and his brother were thrown into jail, but before they could be charged, a mob broke into their cell and killed them both.

The newspaper Smith attacked had been exposing the Mormon practice of polygamy, which is a central tenet of their faith and one of the reasons they have attracted such widespread hostility. **Brigham Young**, Smith's successor, fathered 56 children with 16 wives. In 1890 polygamy was outlawed in the US, a condition that was imposed on the Mormons by the federal authorities to allow them to form their own state, but fundamentalists continued to practise it despite threats of excommunication.

In recent years, polygamy has made a comeback amongst Mormons, with breakaway groups setting up their own churches to recognise plural marriages. In 1998 the London *Sunday Times* reported that polygamy has more practitioners amongst Mormons in America today (around 35,000, including family members) than in the nineteenth century.

Modern Cults

'In the event of the rapture, this car will be unmanned' reads a bumper sticker in the US midwest. As the year 2000 approaches, belief in the forthcoming apocalypse has moved beyond the realms of religious fundamentalism and into everyday life, tapping into basic concerns about the fate of the world. Issues such as nuclear war, population growth and

the global ecological crisis have become the present-day equivalents of the plagues, famines and wars that fanned apocalyptic flames in the Middle Ages.

The millennial myth still retains a powerful hold on the imagination, adapting to the idioms of the age: fundamentalists believe that angels descending from heaven will save the faithful, but for other eschatological cults the apocalypse will be followed by the descent of gods in spacecraft, to save believers who have reached a higher plane of consciousness.

Detailed below are some of the better known postwar millennialist movements and cults. They are unlikely to be the last. In the US, the **Cult Awareness Network** warns of a new wave of doomsday cults committing mass suicide as the millennium approaches.

Aetherius Society

The **Aetherius Society** was formed by London taxi-driver **George King** in 1955 after he heard a mysterious voice telling him he had been selected by the 'Cosmic Masters' to become a spokesman for the 'Interplanetary Parliament' who would soon usher in a utopian age on earth. King channeled messages claiming that the Star of Bethlehem was a flying saucer which had brought Jesus to earth, and that Jesus and other religious leaders such as Rama-Krishna and Buddha are now living on Venus.

Aetherians believe that the world is in great danger but catastrophe has been averted many times thanks to their efforts in storing thousands of hours of prayer in special 'radionic batteries', based on gold and crystals, which are used to release spiritual energy at times of crisis. His Eminence Sir George King, the great Aquarian Master, left the physical world on July 12, 1997 'to return to his true spiritual home amongst the great ones'.

Raëlians

The **Raëlians'** central belief is that life on earth was created by aliens known as the **Elohim**. The cult was launched by a former sports journalist, **Claude Vorilhon**, who claims that the Elohim abducted his mother, inseminated her and then erased her memory of the experience. Vorilhon changed his name to Raël, claiming to be the last in a long line of prophets, when his mission (and his origins) were revealed to him in the 1970s. Raël claims that we have entered the 'age of apocalypse', and after the cataclysm the Elohim will descend to save those who have entered a higher plane of consciousness.

Combining New Age and doomsday beliefs, the movement claims to have around 35,000 members (mostly in Europe and the US) who are required to tithe 10 percent of their income to Raël. In the past the Raëlians have attracted controversy due to the overtly sexual nature of some of their practices, notably 'sensual meditations' intended to banish adherents' sense of Judaeo-Christian guilt, which take place at 'courses of awakening' in discreet rural locations.

More recently, the cult announced that they were offering a service giving infertile or gay couples the chance to have a child cloned from one of them in laboratories which the Raëlians are building for this purpose. Launching **'Clonaid'** in late 1997, Raël said that "cloning will enable mankind to reach eternal life".

Branch Davidians

The siege at Waco, Texas, in 1993 in which at least 85 members of the **Branch Davidian** sect died is one of the most recent examples of a doomsday cult whose apocalyptic beliefs turned into a self-fulfilling prophecy. The Branch Davidians, a breakaway group from the mainstream Seventh-Day Adventists, established a centre at Waco in 1935, naming it Mount Carmel. In 1959 they predicted the end of the world and the resurrection of the faithful; hundreds gathered on the appointed day, but the hour merely passed them by.

The sect languished until the late 1980s, when a 'semi-literate rock guitarist' called **Vernon Howell** took over as leader. Howell, who later changed his name to **David Koresh**, had a hugely detailed knowledge of the Bible and reinvigorated the sect with his beliefs, in particular that the prophecy of the 'Seven Seals' was now being fulfilled and that the apocalypse was imminent. He fortified Mount Carmel and started stockpiling automatic weapons. This attracted the attention of the Bureau of Alcohol, Tobacco and Firearms (ATF), who mounted an ill-conceived raid on February 28, 1993 in which four ATF agents were killed. A full-scale siege began, ending 51 days later when the authorities rammed the compound with tanks, causing a conflagration in which Koresh and most of his followers perished.

Aum Shinrikyo

Aum Shinrikyo ('Aum Supreme Truth') is a Japanese doomsday cult that hit the world headlines in March 1995 when its members released clouds of deadly Sarin gas in sixteen stations of the Tokyo subway, killing twelve people and putting 5500 in hospital. A series of raids on 25 Aum centres around Japan unveiled stockpiles of chemicals and AK-47 automatic rifles; the cult had already bought a Russian helicopter and was planning to buy tanks.

With around 10,000 followers at the time of the 1995 attack, the cult was led by a half-blind guru, **Shoko Asahara**, whose doctrines combined yoga, Buddhism and

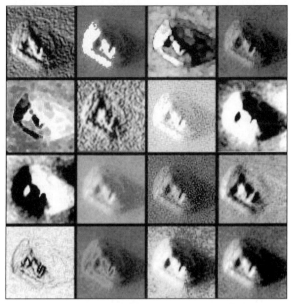

western apocalyptic tendencies. Asahara had used LSD and truth serum on his followers (who were required to wear strange headsets) and had murdered more than a hundred of them, using a cement grinder to dispose of their bones. Asahara is currently in prison, but in late 1997 it was reported that Aum Shinrikyo is still recruiting new members and that cult priests are predicting in their lectures that Armageddon will take place within two years.

Order of the Solar Temple

Alongside the events precipitated by Aum Shinrikyo, the activities of the **Order of the Solar Temple** rank amongst the most shocking of the cult dramas during the 1990s. Founded in the 1980s, the cult claimed to trace its lineage back to the medieval legend of the Knights Templar, and its ceremonies involved elaborate rituals with robes and swords. Its leader, **Luc Jouret**, believed that the world was about to undergo a massive environmental disaster, and that this was the apocalypse foretold in Revelation. Those who joined the Order would be saved and lifted off across space to the star Sirius, where they would be reincarnated as 'Christ-like solar beings'.

The cult, originally based in Switzerland and Canada, first hit the headlines in September 1994. In Canada, a young couple and their baby were ritually murdered, after which other cult members set up a petrol bomb which burned them all alive. A few hours later fire broke out at the cult's farm-house in Switzerland, and police discovered an underground chapel with 22 bodies arranged in a circle around an altar; nineteen had been shot, and three suffocated. Shortly after-wards, two more petrol bombs exploded in Swiss ski chalets, and 25 more bodies were discovered.

One of the documents left behind by the cult stated that 'the initiates who are evolved enough...will now voluntarily leave this world and reach the Absolute Dimension of Truth. They are in fact helped to escape a fate of destruction now awaiting the whole wicked world in a matter of months, if not weeks'.

Sixteen more cult members died in 1995 in the French Alps, and a further five in Canada in March 1997. On January 8, 1998, the Spanish police arrested 31 cult members in Tenerife just hours before they planned to follow their leader to the 3718m summit of the Tiede mountain on the island in order to commit mass suicide, in the belief that the world was to end at 8pm that day. The group, believed to have been an offshoot of the Order of the Solar Temple, told police that a spaceship would land to collect their souls and transport them to another planet.

Heaven's Gate

On March 22, 1997, 39 members of a cult known as **Heaven's Gate** committed mass suicide in a San Diego mansion. Cult members 'exited' their bodies ('vehicles') with the help of phenobarbitol, vodka and suffocation with plastic bags, believing they were on their way to join a spaceship travelling in the wake of the comet **Hale-Bopp**.

The cult was led by self-styled guru **Marshall Herff Applewhite** (known as 'Do'), and its doctrine was a bizarre cocktail of apocalyptic Christianity, New Age mysticism and alien-abduction lore. It was the Christian heritage updated for the science fiction age: Mary was impregnated on a spacecraft, and the aliens were returning to beam up believers to the 'level above human'.

Despite the cultic UFO trappings, the cornerstone of the Heaven's Gate worldview was the mainstream apocalyptic belief that has dominated American evangelism for over a century.

HALE-BOPP Brings Closure to:

HEAVEN'S GATE

As was promised - the keys to Heaven's Gate are here again in Ti and Do (The UFO Two) as they were in Jesus and His Father 2000 yrs. ago.

Books

Many of the books listed below are in print and in paper-back – those that are out of print (o/p) should be easy to track down in secondhand bookshops. Publishers follow each title; first the UK publisher, then the US. Only one publisher is listed if the UK and US publishers are the same. Where books are published in only one of these countries, UK or US comes after the publisher's name.

Futuristic

Adrian Berry, *The Next 500 Years: Life in the Coming Millennium* (Headline; W H Freeman & Co; 1995). Looking ahead to cities on Mars, terraforming planets, the storage of human personalities on disk, three-million tonne bombs which can blow up planets, and other fantasies.

Marshall T Savage, *The Millennial Project: Colonising the Galaxy in Eight Easy Steps* (Little, Brown; Empyrean; 1992). The whole process begins with the growth of oceanic cities, followed by building a bridge into space, establishing habitable eco-spheres on other planets, colonising the moon, transmuting solar matter and finally going to live on the stars. What could be simpler?

History & Millenarian Movements

Felipe Ferna'ndez-Armesto, *Millennium: A History of Our Last Thousand Years* (Bantam; Touchstone; 1995). A monumental (830-page) and idiosyncratic work that charts the shifting influence of cultures over the centuries. The author argues that the historical initiative in human affairs originated in the Far East, from where it passed to 'Atlantic civilisation' with the rise of capitalism, and is now shifting back to the Pacific Rim.

Asa Briggs and Daniel Snowman (eds), *Fins de Siècle: How Centuries End 1400–2000* (Yale University Press, US; 1996). Six eminent historians each examine a century's end (starting in 1390) and reflect on the prevailing consciousness of time. They conclude that a 'sense of ending' seems to have pervaded each period studied – and with good reason – since epoch-making events have tended to be clustered around the turn of centuries, but otherwise the essays (originally part of a radio series) fail to hang together in any meaningful way.

Norman Cohn, *The Pursuit of the Millennium* (Pimlico; Oxford University Press; 1978). A classic of scholarship, Cohn's often-cited work examines the revolutionary millenarians and mystical anarchists of the Middle Ages.

Michael Grosso, *The Millennium Myth: Love and Death at the End of Time* (Quest; Theosophical Publishing House; 1995). Michael Grosso's book follows a well-trodden route in tracing the history of apocalyptic and millennial visions from biblical and medieval times through to contemporary cults and the New Age movement, but he parts company with more objective accounts in his belief that 'forces are awakening everywhere, propelling humanity to powerful transformation'. He has in fact fallen for the millennium myth.

Philip Lamy, *Millennium Rage: Survivalists, White Supremacists and the Doomsday Prophecy* (Plenum Press, US; 1996). A perceptive and illuminating book that links the rise of the far-right militias, white supremacists and other 'survivalist' cults to the apocalyptic and millennial traditions in mainstream American culture and religion. Lamy's disturbing analysis sheds light on phenomena such as the Unabomber, the Branch Davidians, and the Oklahoma bombers to show how they have distorted apocalyptic symbolism to their own ends, gearing up for Armageddon in this world rather than the next.

Damian Thompson, *The End of Time: Faith and Fear in the Shadow of the Millennium* (Sinclair-Stevenson; University Press of New England; 1996). One of the best books published on contemporary millenarian cults, this thoughtful analysis traces the millennial time-line from the Bible through medieval movements to Aum Skinrikyo, Waco and the Atlanta bombings. Thompson must be peeved that Heaven's Gate occurred too late for inclusion (no doubt that will be remedied in further editions), especially since it confirmed his own prognosis on the impact of the Internet on apocalyptic belief, which turned out to be spot-on.

Prophecy

John Hogue, *The Millennium Book of Prophecy* (HarperCollins; 1994). Features 777 visions and predictions from Nostradamus, Edgar Cayce, Gurdjieff, Madame Blavatsky and many others.

A T Mann, *Millennium Prophecies: Predictions for the Year 2000* (Element Books, UK; 1992). Encompasses everything from pyramidology to Aquarian predictions.

James Manning, *Prophecies for the New Millennium* (Thames and Hudson, UK; 1997). Beautifully produced and illustrated with a striking series of original collages, this compact compendium romps through all the main strands of millennial prophecy and predicts an era of galactic harmony brought about by the arrival of the Age of Aquarius, the turning of the Buddhist Wheel of Dharma, and the advent of the Hindu 'Krita Yuga', the Age of Gold.

Stefan Paulus, *Nostradamus 2000: Who Will Survive?* (Michael O'Mara Books, UK; 1997). One of the best of the current crop of Nostradamus books.

Stephen Skinner, *Millennium Prophecies* (Virgin Books; 1994). A large-format, highly illustrated guide that leads down some fairly idiosyncratic paths concerning prophecies over the centuries.

Religion

Harold Bloom, *Omens of Millennium* (Fourth Estate; Riverhead Books; 1997). A fascinating study of gnosticism, angelology, and dreams through several centuries of religious thought, and their relationship to the approaching millennium. According to Bloom, 65 percent of Americans believe in angels, and he predicts that 'angels will be at least partially restored to their equivocal glory as the millennium nears'.

Robert G. Clouse (ed), *The Meaning of the Millennium: Four Views* (InterVarsity Press; 1977). Four theologians debate the significance of Christian millennial texts.

Michael Drosnin, *The Bible Code* (Weidenfeld & Nicolson; Simon & Schuster; 1997). Controversial bestseller that claims to have cracked a code 'buried' in the Bible which foretells events thousands of years after it was written, including the assassination of Yitzhak Rabin in 1995. The book's apocalyptic predictions will no doubt fuel millennium fever amongst those gullible enough to believe it.

Science and Time

Nicholas Campion, *The Great Year: Astrology, Millenarianism and History in Western Tradition* (Penguin Books; 1994). An important and often-quoted study on the links between concepts of linear and cyclical time and societies' views of their place in the cosmos, this scholarly work (700 pages, with almost 100 pages of notes and references) is not for the faint-hearted.

Stephen Jay Gould, *Questioning the Millennium: A Rationalist's Guide to a Precisely Arbitrary Countdown* (Jonathan Cape; Thomas T. Beeler; 1997). Bearing all the usual erudite hallmarks of Gould's questioning mind, this elegantly written little volume explores the religious and rational roots of our fascination with the millennium and our compulsion to impose time-schemes on the universe. The last chapter is particularly compelling: it relates the story of an idiot savant who, like Dustin Hoffman in *Rain Man*, has the power to instantaneously calculate dates deep into the past and the future. The identity of this young man, whose gift is but an offshoot of the curse of autism, is revealed in a moving peroration.

Simon Reeve and Colin McGhee, *The Millennium Bomb* (Vision
   Paperbacks; 1996). The first in-depth analysis of the millennium
   time bomb problem to appear in book form.

Margo Westrheim, *Calendars of the World: A Look at Calendars
   & the Way We Celebrate* (Oneworld Publications; 1993). A good
   introduction to the numerous solutions to the problem of
   measuring time from different cultures around the world, and the
   associated rituals and festivities.

THE MILLENNIUM

DIRECTORIES

The Millennium
on the Internet

The millennium could have been tailor-made for cyber-space, or vice versa. The global scale of the celebrations about to take place has been echoed on the Internet's **World Wide Web and Newsgroups**, which are littered with millennial visions and plans, reflecting the collective fascination with the arrival of the year 2000.

The Internet is a natural home for conspiracy theorists, doomsday merchants, UFO enthusiasts, eco-prophets and believers in the 'end-times', all of whom are having a field day in the uncensored realms of cyberspace. The flip side of the coin, the dawning of a New Age, and how best to transform the world into a twenty-first century utopia, also occupies gigabytes of the network. Other preoccupations that emerge include the millennium time bomb (Y2K) problem, and far too many fruitless debates about when the millennium actually starts.

Plenty of opportunists are attempting to float money-making millennium schemes, many of them doomed to failure, but a lot of fun ideas have also emerged for parties, celebrations and general mayhem as the big date approaches. You'll also find some first-rate sites on topics such as time and calendars, and studies of millennial cults.

The listings that follow are just a selection of millennial Web sites we found interesting. Depending on which search engine you use, a hit on 'millennium' can yield anything between 200,000 and 370,000 hits ('apocalypse' brings up 80,000 matches, and 'doomsday' a respectable 24,000).

There is plenty more to discover by following the links on the pages listed here. As with any Web guide, however, usual caveats apply: the Web is nothing if not a fast-changing environment, and Web addresses can change, move or disappear with alarming regularity.

General Sites and Events

Club2000

http://www.club2000.com/

Includes news, Webstore (books and videos), a kids' section and
a twenty-first century 'adobe house' built from steel and
compressed hay.

Earth Day

http://www.envirolink.org/earthday

Explains the genesis of Earth Day and how you can get involved
locally, with links to different countries and world regions.

E.A.R.T.H renewal walks

http://www.rain.org/#planetwk/erwalks1.html

Join in the various E.A.R.T.H (Educational Arts and
Resourceful Technologies for Humanity) renewal walks taking
place in the run-up to the millennium.

Everything 2000

http://www.everything2000.com

One of the best nonspecialist sites, with up-to-date news briefs
on topics such as travel and the millennium, parties, and a
comprehensive set of links to peace movements, civic
campaigns, religion and other areas.

Millennium Alliance

http://www.igc.apc.org/millennium/alliance/index.html

The Millennium Alliance for 'Peace, Justice and Sustainability'
was founded in 1996 as a project of the Millennium Institute.
Their pages contain a huge volume of data on what they call
'threshold observances' taking place around the world,
categorised by types of event, country, region and city.

Millennium Concentrate

http://home.earthlink.net/~hipbone/MilCon.html

An excellent reference point, with brief summaries and links to
sites concerning comparative religion, cults, end-timers and
much more.

Millennium's Eve Parties: The International Register

http://www.jepa.co.uk/shopping/party.html

This site has developed into an entertaining list of public, private and commercial parties, with proposals and suggestions as varied as scuba diving on the Great Barrier Reef to a twelve-hour trance rave in South Africa and Hogmanay in Fort Henry, Lake Ontario.

Millennium Portal

http:www.skywebs.com/earthportals/milenport.html

A selection of links to 'ideas, solutions and predictions of what lies ahead...at the portal to the twenty-first century'.

Millennium Society

http://www.millenniumsociety.org/

The Millennium Society claims to be one of the first organisations established to celebrate the year 2000. The cornerstone of their plans is a party at the Great Pyramids, linked by live broadcasts to a series of other celebrations worldwide.

New Year's Eve 1999

http://users.mwci.net/lapoz~/1999.html

Suggests books, films, poems and even food to celebrate with, plus contributions from individuals about where they'd like to be – some of them pretty daft.

Odyssey 2000

http://www.cortland.com/bike_expo/kneeland/kneeland.html

Information on routes, participants, fees and other aspects of the Odyssey 2000 round-the-world bike ride.

Project Millennium

http://www3.mistral.co.uk/ruzz/about.htm

A flyer to put on a 'massive concert' in the UK, followed by a Concorde flight to the US and another 'massive concert' in New York. Fundraising events staged so far include a disco on Worthing Pier...keep dreaming, guys.

Project 21st century

http://www.webhelp.com/future.htm

Broad-ranging links to articles on the theme of 'what does the global community think the twenty-first century will bring?'

River 2000

http://www.river2000.co.uk/

Planned as the first expedition ever to 'transnavigate' the world by the rivers, lakes, canals and the inland seas of Eurasia, North America, South America and Africa, River 2000 will also conduct a series of scientific and environmental surveys that will link into a schools' education programme.

Talk2000

http://hcol.humberc.on.ca/talk2000.htm

Jay Gary's site covers a wealth of material relating to millennium movements, from folklore and festivities to the darker side of cults. His 'Let's Talk 2000' newsletter is also a useful resource on what's going on around the world in the run-up to 2000.

The Billennium

http://www.rust.net/~mc2000/

Home page of a planned three-day extravaganza at 24 'historic sites' in 24 time zones.

**Around the World...
a Cast of Billions™**

The Electronic Millennium Project

http://emp2000.ukonline.co.uk/

Users are invited to join this Web-based enterprise to celebrate the millennium, currently still in its formative stages.

Apocalypse and Prophecy

Cybotron: the Cyber Lord Apocalypse Project

http://pages.prodigy.com/cybotron

A potent brew of weird music, apocalyptic texts and sexual imagery. Strange indeed.

Futurecast

http://www.futurefate.com/

An assemblage of a wide variety of predictions, from Hopi prophecies to geological catastrophes.

Millennium Fever

http://www.crawford.com/media.maniacs/media.html

 Marc Aramian lets his imagination rip with a series of apocalyptic postings from the future, 'received sporadically' from the renegade cyberwarrior Gabriel who is caught up in a world at war in the year 2000.

Millennium I: Our Times

http://www.aquarianage.org/

Predicts Armaggedon at Christmas 1999 followed by a renaissance in 2004. Typical cyber-crackpot stuff.

Nostradamus Society of America

http://www.nostradamus.com/

Predicts warfare in July of 1999 according to one of only seven of Nostradamus's quatrains that contain actual dates.

Prophecy, Earth Changes and the Millennium

http:/www.are-cayce.com/millen.htm

One of several articles based on the prophecies of the late Edgar Cayce, from the Web site of the Association for Research and

Enlightenment at the Atlantic University in Virginia Beach which he founded.

Top Ten Prophecies for the Year 2000
http://www.aa.net/~mwm/atlantis/issue2/ar2topten.html

From Revelation to the secrets of the Pyramids, this brief summary is from issue 2 of *Atlantis Rising*.

Christian

All the World Sing Praise
http://www2.tilehill.ac.uk/~stu1/

All the World Sing Praise/1 Jan 2000 is a project of the Catholic Youth Ministry Faith Alive in the UK to create a Songs of Praise event in every capital of the world for the first day of the next millennium.

Jubilee 2000
http://www.xibalba.com/xibalba/solt/jubilee/2000.html

Unofficial Jubilee 2000 Web site with links to other Christian sites.

The Rapture Truth Home Page
http://users.cyberzone.net/siscokid/

Christian Scientists' page declaring that even Christians will not be saved from the Great Tribulation.

The Timeline from 750 AD to 250 years into the Millennium
http://www.cynet.com/Jesus/timelin4.htm

Verily, the Empire of the Antichrist is about to be established, the US and Russia will be destroyed in the Battle of Armageddon, and in the year 2000 (give or take a few years) Jesus will set up an Earthly Kingdom for his Millennial Reign. The Fundamentalist take on events.

Third Millennium & Jubilee Year 2000
http://www.nccbuscc.org/jubilee/vatican/prayer.htm

Official Web site from the National Conference of Catholic Bishops detailing the preparation for and celebration of the Jubilee Year 2000 in the United States.

Cults and Conspiracies

Links to right-wing bozos and extremists on WWW
http://www.execpc.com/~awallace/bozolink.html

Just as it says, offering a chilling insight into the mentality of numerous right-wing millennial groups.

Planetary Activation Organisation
http://www.paoweb.com/

Echoes of the Unarius Academy of Science and Heaven's Gate from the Planetary Activation Organisation (formerly the Ground Crew Project), who are preparing for mass landings of 15.5 million spaceships from the Galactic Federation.

60 Great Conspiracies of All Time
http://www.mille.org/sites.html

An entertaining trawl through latter-day conspiracy theories, from the apocalyptic significance of Hale-Bopp to the demise of TWA flight 800 and more.

The MJ Project
http://www.mj-millennium.org/text/whatis.html

The aim of the project is to cover the US with a forest of 250 million marijuana plants (an average of 67 per square mile of the country) in 2000, thus forcing the government to legalise dope in the face of this gigantic crop. The project urges fellow tokers (there are an estimated ten million in the US) to save their seeds and scatter them in likely locations on April 20, 2000.

UFOs, Aliens, Mars and Antichrist
http://www.geocities.com/Area51/Vault/3040/

The Watcher Ministry's pages claim that Satan was exiled to Mars and that UFOs are controlled by the fallen Sons of God. Other pages lead into detailed studies of biblical texts.

Unarius Academy of Science
http://www.serve.com/unarius/

UFO group who believe that the Space Brothers from the Pleiadean cluster of planets will land their starship on a rising portion of Atlantis in the Bermuda Triangle in the year 2001. Wonderful wacky stuff.

Virtual Suicide Cult
http://www.ArsNova.org/vmall/vcult.html

It had to happen...'with our popular new programme, there's no need to suffer the incovenience and expense of belonging to a full-time, live-in suicide cult'. For only US$99 (£69) you can also be reincarnated in an eastern metaphysical cult, South American Indian cult and so on.

Music, Media and the Arts

Big Opera Mundi
http://www.quadrant.net/bom2000/

Big Opera Mundi (BOM) plans to stage a live 'great world opera' with artists from all over the globe connected via the Internet to create a 24-hour symphony.

Millennium

http://members.aol.com/monica725/millen.htm

http://members.aol.com/monica725/millen.htm#Millennium Synopsis

Discussion group for Chris Carter's TV series 'Millennium'.

Millennium Arts

http://www.art1.com/

Nice-looking site with a gallery of selected New Age-type images from various artists.

Millennium Celebrations

http://www.2000celebration.com/

Another flyer, this time for a 'worldwide, simultaneous and orchestrated five-day extravaganza', with 'world-renowned entertainment' to usher in the next 1000 years.

Millennium Midnight

http://lama.cnam.fr/millennium/mmfr01.html

A proposal for artists from around the world to take part in the creation of a joint artwork, via the Internet, each joining in at midnight in their own time zone and then relaying the results on to the next. The result will be published on the Net and as a CD-rom.

Millennium Project24

http://web-star.com/millennium/project.html

Flyer for a planned live TV broadcast on January 1, 2000, covering 24 hours of celebrations around the globe.

Millennium Renaissance

http://www.well.com/user/tcircus/Cyberlab7/index.html

San Francisco's CyberLab 7 prepares for the millennium with online 'visual realities' and the development of 'planet change projects'.

Millennium Time Machine
http://www.comlab.ox.ac.uk/archive/other/museums/mda/mill.htm

The Millennium Time Machine (MTM) aims to digitalise Britain's museum collections and to put them on-line to the nation's schools, libraries, homes and to the world.

Sculpture for Jubilee 2000
http://www.jorlando.com/JUB.htm

Sculptor Joe Orlando proposes a 135ft-high 'hyper-parabolic column' covered in panels depicting the Life of Christ.

The New Millennium
http://www.garfnet.org.uk/new_mill

British e-zine with good links and articles on the millennium bug.

World Action for the Millennium
http://www.wam2000.org/index.html

Explains the thinking and operational plans behind WAM's scheme to link the inhabitants of the earth to share a musical message on January 1, 2000.

World Millennium Snapshot
http://users.mwci.net~lapoz/1999Snap.html

An invitation to contribute towards making the turn of the century the most photographed and videographed moment in history.

New Age

Being Millennial
http://www.geocities.com/

Fairly extensive links through the 'philosophies of the third millennium [and] resources to help guide your path into the next age of humankind', including mysticism, prophecies, UFOs and spiritual pages.

Calendersign
http://web.vip.at/calendersign/

An Austrian site aimed at raising awareness of the dawning of the Age of Aquarius (from an 'archaeo-astronomical' standpoint).

Their pages include several zodiac graphs, essays, a bibliography (German only), and an on-line shop where you can order their symbolic 1000-day Countdown Calendar.

Global Visions
http://www.globalvisions.org/

A clearinghouse for information about 'spiritual and humanitarian activity on the planet'.

Millennium Matters
http://www.m-m.org/jz/intro.html

Another general links page with some in-depth reviews, encompassing a very broad definition of what constitutes 'millennium matters' (reviews of a herb gardening site, for instance, stretches 'millennial' beyond the point where it makes sense). Also includes Matters of Spirit links, the Sphinx Group links, Gaia Alert links, Uformation links, and Vision of Sanctuary links.

Omega
http://deoxy.org/omega.htm

Entertaining and eclectic site covering Gaia, Hopi prophecies, and futuristic thinking. Good graphics.

2001: Journey to the Next Millennium
http://www.sun2001.com/

Billed as a 'full service metaphysical site', the Web Prophet's pages include features on reincarnation, astrology, runes, the tarot and 'transformation', as well as offering psychic counselling by e-mail ('secure credit card charge') and rune jewellery.

Peace Movements

Great Millennium Peace Ride
http://www.holistic.satori.net.au/gmpr/index.html#info

Describes the aims and goals of the GMPR, with quotes from intended participants, sponsorship information and route details.

Peace 2000

http://www.peaceday.org/

How and when to join in the call for world peace. Includes links to the Earth Rainbow Network, Peace 2000 Proclamation, campaigns to ban landmines and more.

Year 2000 Campaign to Redirect World Military Spending to Human Development

http://www.fas.org/pub/gen/mswg/year2000/

Initiated in 1995, the campaign hopes to involve all countries in talks to reduce armaments by the year 2000.

Publications and Studies

A Catalog for the End of Time

http://www.rmharris.com/pub/abaa-booknet/catalogs/krowncat/intro.html

Beverly Hills bookseller Krown & Spellman's on-line catalogue. Lists with synopses of hundreds of antiquarian books (at decidedly contemporary prices) on topics such as geomancy, mythology, cults, witchcraft, alchemy, occult sciences and millenarianism.

Armageddon Books

http://www.armageddonbooks.com/

On-line bookstore with a huge range of stock covering everything connected to Bible prophecy from premillennialism to Middle East current affairs, the Rapture and the Antichrist. Also features a prophecy chat room and links to prophecy sites on the Web.

Center for Millennial Studies

http://www.mille.org/

Explains the functions of the Center for Millennial Studies and carries some thoughtful analyses of millennial and apocalyptic movements. Good links pages, with sites differentiated according to various shades of apocalyptic beliefs. Also has a comprehensive on-line bookstore for millennium-related titles.

First Millennial Foundation
http://www.millennial.org/

Web site of Marshall T Savage's book of the same name, with links to FMF Chapters in the US and UK, discussion groups, newsletters, projects and articles relating to his theory that we should create space colonies in the oceans before venturing off the planet.

Millennia Monitor
http:www.fas.org/2000/index.html

The Federation of American Scientists (FAS) set out a framework for monitoring apocalyptic groups. Includes links to other pages studying millennial movements.

Millennium Publications
http://gnp1.com/

On-line sci-fi and fantasy magazine.

Millennium Whole Earth Catalog
http://www.well.net/mwec/home.html

'Integrating the best tools from the past 25 years with the best tools for the next 25 years', the Catalog takes its original inspiration (communities, self-help, and whole systems) into cyberspace, providing access to resources and ideas on everything from the environment to telecommunications in the next millennium.

National Millennium Foundation
http://www.tmn.com/~renfro/M3.htm

The Washington-based National Millennium Foundation's home page. Proposes various projects, including educational initiatives and 'lunar fireworks'.

The Millennium Conference
http://www.omnimag.com/archives/features/millennium/conference/

Extracts from papers given at The Millennium Conference held in New York in November 1996, hosted by *Omni* magazine.

The Millennium Institute
http://www.igc.org/millennium

Outlines the work of the Millennium Institute, with updates on current projects. Formerly the Institute for Twenty First Century Studies, the Institute aims to promote 'long-term, integrated global thinking' to create sustainable lifestyles for the next millennium. The site includes links to events and papers by millennial scholars.

The Millennium International Research Project
http://members.tripod.com/~MillenniumProject/intro

A research project undertaken by UCLA to find out what people around the world think about the end of one millennium and the beginning of another. You can participate (anonymously) by e-mail.

The Millennium Watch Institute
http://www.channel1.com/mpr/mpr.html

The Millennium Watch Institute's pages contain a series of objective, in-depth features on various millennial cults from back issues of their Millennium Prophecy Report. Founder Ted Daniels is one of the foremost authorities on millennial cults in the US, and this site is well worth browsing.

The Skeptical Inquirer
http://www.csicop.org/si/

Extracts from the Skeptical Inquirer, published by the Committee for the Scientific Investigation of Claims of the Paranormal. Insightful analyses on topics such as Heaven's Gate, UFO mythology and so on.

Time and Calendars

A Walk Through Time
http://physics.nist.gov/GenInt/Time/time.html

Appealing pages from the US National Institute of Standards and Technology (NIST) that go back to basic explanations of calendars, clocks, atomic time and world time scales.

Bill Hollon's well-presented and comprehensive site on time and calendars
http://www.greenheart.com/billh/

Not a particularly snappy title, but accurate enough.

Calendarland
http://www.juneau.com/home/janice/calendarland/millennium/

An excellent resource with links to almost everything conceivable connected to calendars – celestial, cultural, religious, interactive, perpetual and Web calendars, to name but a few.

Exactly when does the new millennium actually arrive anyway?
http://www.mohawk.net/~barbaria/millennium.html

Heavy-going, verbose trawl through the date problem. Suggests we move the date forward so that the year 2000 coincides with the birth date of Christ. Could be a spoof if it showed any traces of irony – but sadly it doesn't.

US Naval Observatory (USNO) Time Service
http://tycho.usno.navy.mil/leap.html

Explains why and how leap seconds are inserted into atomic time, or Universal Time Coordinated (UTC). Also contains data on adjusting Loran-C, GPS and Omega systems.

When does the Millennium begin?
http://www.igc.apc.org/millennium/begins.html

The Millennium Institute's answer is that whether you pick the year 2000 or 2001 to celebrate, we will be in a wider 'millennial moment' from 1999–2001 which should be used as a fulcrum for constructive change.

Yahoo! Calendars

http://www.yahoo.com/text/Reference/Calendars/

Good compilation of links to calendar sites.

Year Zero Campaign

http://members.aol.com/go2zero/index.htm

Home page of the people who want to wind the calendar back to zero at the beginning of the next millennium.

Year 2000 'Time Bomb' Web sites

Millennium Date Corporation

http://www.milleniumdate.co.uk/main.htm

Commercial site for Y2K solutions.

RightTime

http://www.RightTime.com/

This site offers a free fix for PC users (DOS v3 or later, IBM OS/2 and Windows except NT). Contains links to diagnostic software that will help you determine if your computer is at risk.

The Good, the Bad and the Ugly

http://www.demon.co.uk/dita/year2000/ye02001.html

Lists PCs that fail the date rollover test and explains how to test yours.

The Mac and the Year 2000

http://devworld.apple.com/dev/technotes/tn/tn1049.html

No problem with Macs, they say – until 2019.

The Year 2000

http://www.zebra.co.uk/workshop/year2000.htm

Includes details on Y2K conferences, as well as listing over 120 'tool vendors' to solve the problem.

The Year 2000 Information Centre

http://www.compinfo.co.uk/y2k.htm

Home page of the Year 2000 Information Centre, run by consultant Peter de Jager, who was one of the first to raise the alarm on the potential scale of the problem. Contains links to dozens of other commercial consultants in the millennium de-bugging business.

Top Ten Reasons for Not Worrying About the Year 2000

http://www.adm.uwaterloo.ca/info1999/top10.html

All the good excuses ('January 1, 2000 is a Saturday and Monday a holiday...you'll have lots of time over the weekend') courtesy of the University of Waterloo. Their Year 2000 Issues and References has more practical links to sources of information (http://www.adm.uwaterloo.ca/info1999/2000ref.html).

Year 2000 Date Transition Issue

http://www.microsoft.com/cio/year.asp

'Microsoft cares deeply about its customers'... and Bill's comprehensive Year 2000 pages tell you everything you might need to know.

Y2K Cinderella Project

http://www.cinderella.co.za/cinder.html

'Dedicated to a fairy tale ending', the Cinderella Project's excellent pages detail a number of zero-cost, minimal-impact solutions and include one of the best links listings for Y2K issues.

Millennium Tours from Britain and the US

As the world prepares for the party of the century, the travel and tourism industry is in a state of disarray. Several tour operators have brought out brochures with special 'millennium tours', but there are many more who haven't even started thinking about it.

What is certain is that many of the world's most exotic locations and luxury hotels will be heavily oversubscribed. London hotels at the top end of the market – such as the *Ritz*, the *Savoy*, and *Claridges* – have been deluged with requests, although no firm plans have yet been announced. Castles in Scotland are in big demand too, even though some are charging up to £10,000 (US$16,500) a night. And it's the same story worldwide, from the US to India, Australia to the Caribbean and, of course, in particular the 'first sunrise' islands of the Pacific.

Most of the tour operators listed here who have published millennium programmes to date are at the top end of the market, with no-expense spared gala nights in Russian palaces, private safaris in Africa, or 'double celebrations' which cross the dateline and allow you to have two New Year's Eve parties. A St Louis-based company, **Intrav**, is even offering a sixteen-day round-the-world trip in Concorde at US$70,000 (£43,000) per person. Cruise companies are also reporting a boom in bookings for the millennium: **Cunard** alone is sitting on around £5 million (US$8.1m) in deposits from would-be clients, and cabins are oversubscribed by more than double the numbers available.

BRITAIN

Abercrombie & Kent are offering a number of options for upmarket safaris and retreats to tropical island hideaways. Their most distinctive package is the Great Africa Air Cruise, which will leave Gatwick on a chartered, 75-seater plane on December 27, 1999 for a two-week private tour calling at Luxor, Nairobi, Zanzibar, the Serengeti and Ngorongoro Crater, celebrating New Year's Eve at a hotel overlooking Victoria Falls ⓣ 0171/730 9600.

All-Ways Pacific is offering a New Year's Eve barbecue at Ayer's Rock as part of a 21-day tour of Australia, departing December 20, 1999 ⓣ 01494/875757.

Arctic Experience features one week in Iceland, including excursions and a New Year's Eve party in Reykjavik ⓣ 01737/218800.

Elegant Resorts is taking bookings for hot-air balloon flights at dawn over the Arizona desert ⓣ 01244/897888.

Encounter Overland is planning a year-long journey with two groups setting off simultaneously, one from Greenwich and one from New Zealand, meeting at the halfway point in Africa. The company will be using their existing overland routes and keeping flights to a minimum; you will also be able to join for short legs of the trip throughout 2000 ⓣ 0171/370 6845.

First Dawn Celebrations features a ten-day trip departing December 26, 1999, which includes a royal banquet in Tonga on New Year's Eve, followed by a flight to Samoa to celebrate all over again ⓣ 0171/272 0412.

First to the Sun is offering places for cyclists of moderate ability on a 625-mile trek which starts on December 17, 1999 in Auckland and finishes in Gisborne in time for the first sunrise. Accommodation is in a mobile tented village ℡ 01903/218176.

Goodwood Travel is offering a three-day trip, travelling on Concorde to Vienna for the Millennium Eve Ball at the imperial Hofburg Palace. The package includes a horse-drawn carriage from your hotel to the ball, a gala banquet, and midnight waltz ℡ 01227/763336.

Jetset's 'double celebration' package to the South Pacific includes gala dinners in Tonga on New Year's Eve and then again in Samoa ℡ 0990/555757.

Journey Latin America will be featuring millennium tours of Brazil, taking in New Year's Eve in Rio ℡ 0181/77 8315.

Scantours is featuring a four-night trip to Lapland which will include one night in the famous Ice Hotel, the world's largest igloo ℡ 0171/839 2927.

Silver Cord Maritime Trust is offering twelve passengers the opportunity to follow Cook's voyages around the Pacific in an 80ft converted trawler which will leave London in September 1999. The crew intend to cross the dateline on January 1, 2000 before proceeding to New Zealand for the America's Cup, and Sydney for the Olympics ℡ 01825/767924.

Steppes East plans a four-night trip to St Petersburg for a millennium ball in one of the royal palaces with a gala dinner, champagne, vodka, ice fountains and entertainment ℡ 01285/810267.

The Millennium Train Company has chartered two Eurostar trains, one starting in Paris and the other in London, which will pass each other as they travel between the capitals on New Year's Eve 1999 as part of a lavish six-day party which will include a black-tie gala at Hampton Court, a ball at La Conciergerie in Paris, and midnight revels on the trains ℡ 01737/223303.

Thomas Cook Holidays features a gala dinner at the Cape Sun International Hotel in Cape Town as part of a six-day millennium tour ℡ 01733/417000.

Travel for the Arts is offering four nights in New York over New Year's 1999, including a gala dinner and opera at the Met ℡ 0171/483 4466.

Travel Portfolio's seventeen-day 'double celebration' tour leaves London on December 27 for Bangkok, Sydney (Christmas Day), Fiji (New Year's Eve) and the Cook Islands (New Year's Eve again) ℡ 01284/762255.

Worldwide Journeys and Expeditions is arranging tours which will include watching the sunrise from high spots such as Mount Kilimanjaro or in the Patagonian mountains ℡ 0171/381 8638.

US

Coastline Travel Advisor features a number of cruises, themed balls on the Queen Mary, and trips to New Zealand ℡ 800/448 2374.

Edutrek is offering millennium tours to Paris and Venice, and Orient Express and Concorde trips ℡ 212/989 0170.

Heritage Study Programs Inc is offering a series of tours to Jerusalem and the Holy Land in 2000 ℡ 800/477 2306.

Himalayan Discovery is planning millennium tours in the Nepalese Himalayas and Tibetan monasteries ℡ 714/771 4360.

JMT Travel is offering a 'double millennium' celebration, leaving Las Vegas on December 26, 1999 for Melbourne and then New Year's Eve in Auckland, followed by a second party back in Las Vegas ℡ 888/568 1999.

Little World Travel has space on the 74-berth Windsong, whose Millennium Cruise will be based around Costa Rica ℡ 415/592 0664.

Nomad Travel Planners are offering the 'Big Five 2000' tours which include trips to the Serengeti, Mount Kenya Safari Club, Rajasthan, and the Galapagos ℡ 907/243 0313 ⓦ http://www.nomad-travel.com/mill.htm

Rex Travel are agents for Abercrombie & Kent's Millennium Tours, as well as golf, heli-hiking and other millennium tours ℡ 800/777 7739.

Travcoa feature a variety of packages for New Year's Eve 1999 including safari tours, a gala dinner in Monte Carlo, a dinner dance in the Ciragan Palace Kempinksi in Istanbul, Nile cruises, and a celebration in the Al Bustan Palace in the Sultanate of Oman ℡ 800/598 1001 ⓦ http://www.costatravel.com/travcoa/trav-mill.html

Travel Club Adventures feature a wide range of options including New Year's Eve in the Ngorongoro, sunrise over the Pyramids, a New Year's Eve gala in Hong Kong, the Imperial Millennium Ball in Vienna, and the Galapagos Islands ℡ 562/592 3157 ⓦ http://www.travelclub.adv.com/page23.html

Travel Well Consultants' Destinations 2000 Collection includes a number of party locations for New Year's Eve 1999 including Mount Kilimanjaro, the Pyramids, Machu Picchu, Antarctica, New Zealand, Sydney, Paris, and pilgrimage centres such as Rome and the Holy Land ℡ 617/340 6794.

INDEX

Picture credits

p.1, 14, 199 National Maritime
         Museum
p.28   David Austin
p.40   Richard Davies/Foster and
         Partners
p.59   Nick Wood/Hayes Davidson
p.71   Nick Wood
p.74   Jeremy Young/Foster and
         Partners
p.77   Foster and Partners

p.78   Mark Edwards/Still Pictures
p.81   Alan Davidson/Earth Centre
p.82   Nicholas Grimshaw and
         Partners
p.89   Nicholas Grimshaw and
         Partners
p.97   Marius Alexander/Unique Events
p.134   Jeroen van Putten
p.141   Brian Lynch/Irish Tourist Board
p.152   Jock Pottle/Esto Photographics

KNOW WHERE YOU'RE GOING?

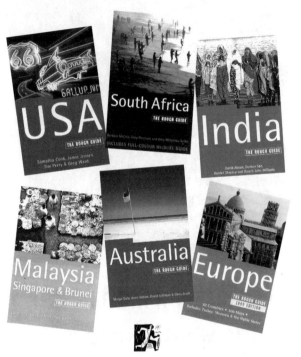

ROUGH GUIDES

*Travel Guides to more than
100 destinations worldwide*